BE
HAPPY
NOW!

From Wall Street Ambition
and the Illusion of Success,
My Path to Happiness

Alison Lanza Falls and
David S. Prudhomme

BALBOA.
PRESS
A DIVISION OF HAY HOUSE

Balboa Press books may be ordered through booksellers or by contacting:

Balboa Press
A Division of Hay House
1663 Liberty Drive
Bloomington, IN 47403
www.balboapress.com
1 (877) 407-4847

Print information available on the last page.

ISBN: 978-1-5043-8416-2 (sc)
ISBN: 978-1-5043-8418-6 (hc)
ISBN: 978-1-5043-8417-9 (e)

Library of Congress Control Number: 2017910843

Balboa Press rev. date: 08/11/2017

Scripture quotations marked NRSV are taken from the New Revised Standard Version of the Bible, Copyright © 1989, by the Division of Christian Education of the National Council of the Churches of Christ in the United States of America. Used by permission. All rights reserved. Website

For Ted, Mary, and David

CONTENTS

Part 1
Three Wake-Up Calls
Hello ... Is Anybody Home?

Part 2
Opening New Doors of My Mind

Part 3
Putting the Lessons into Practice

FOREWORD

By David S. Prudhomme

Your vision will become clear only
when you look into your heart.
Who looks outside, dreams.
Who looks inside, awakens.

—Carl Jung

I remember the day in 2010 when Alison walked into my office for the first time. Through our conversations it was clear she was ready to change her life perceptions and begin the amazing journey of finding her truth, her passion, and her joy. I thought Alison would be a great candidate for "The Best Me NOW!, the proprietary program I had created to guide people to experience their full potential—physically, mentally, and emotionally.

As the founder and director of Mederi Wellness, I have helped thousands of people understand how their minds work, the relationship of the conscious and the subconscious mind, and how they can create positive changes in their lives that are immediate and ongoing. Through my proven program "The Best Me NOW!" people can view their world as a new place, taking back control of their lives, releasing their fears, and transcending their negative and limiting beliefs.

Alison Falls did, and you can too.

As you read our book, you will witness a story of a personal transformation. You will see that true positive change is not only possible but also that it follows a specific path of perception, awareness, and choice. This book is an example of what a life transformation can look like and how you can find your own path to happiness.

You will recognize the journey is the same for everyone. Although your specific life circumstances, experiences, or challenges may be different than Alison's, the transformational process and the steps along the path are the same for all of us.

The steps along the path are the same for all of us because happiness exists within each of us. Most people look outside of themselves—for material things, the right relationship, a new job or career, greater financial success, a new house, etc. They think happiness is something to be attained in the future. Most people live in unhappiness while seeking happiness.

The seven essential steps in this process of going within, which we all must take, are as follows:

1. Learn exactly how your mind and body work together so you can take back control of your autonomic nervous system. This allows you to let go of physical and mental stress.

2. Learn how to choose your emotions rather than react to the people and situations around you.

3. Learn how to rewire your neural networks for success and take back control of your thoughts.

4. Learn how to let go of negative or limiting beliefs about yourself and release any fears.

5. Learn how to change your behavior to achieve your full potential.

6. Reshape the lens of your perception of yourself and your life situation. This leads to positive change in every relationship in your life, personally and professionally.

7. Discover the true purpose of your life—physically, mentally, and emotionally.

True, positive transformation is not only possible, but it also follows this specific path of perception, awareness, and choice.

The process is designed to help you change how you think, feel, and behave *now* ... not tomorrow. Be happy *now*, not next week, not when you have *this* ... or achieve *that*. *Be Happy NOW!*

PREFACE

One cold spring evening at dinner with David, the outline of my book appeared on a napkin. I am not talking about a miracle here. Rather it is an example of how I learn my lessons at a deeper level when I'm challenged to discover what I already know. It is also an example of David's philosophy of serving as a guide, which is very different from playing the role of instructor or teacher.

After six months, as my sessions with David were coming to a close, David asked a simple question. "Have you ever thought of writing a book?"

Intuitively, I blurted out, "Yes!" Indeed, I had thought for a long time about writing a book. I had been thinking about writing a book about moving Aunt Mary. I had moved Aunt Mary, my other mother, four times in five years, and I had become her primary caregiver. I was losing her to the progressive stages of dementia.

As I thought about the book, the focus shifted from my journey with Aunt Mary to my journey to find happiness within me, drawing on my sessions with David, our conversations, my meditations and my daily journal. I was excited!

Over dinner David and I were discussing my story and the lessons I had learned. Midway through dinner I started pressing David, "What do you think about this title or that title? What is the outline for the book?" I was all business. I was approaching the dinner as a meeting, planning and scheduling. "Here are some of my thoughts on the chapters and chapter titles." I was all about the structure of the book, creating a framework so I could start writing.

Every time I asked a question on the form or structure of the book, David answered with a question. "What do you think you learned? First, you need to answer *that* question. Then the outline will appear."

I was getting a little frustrated. "David, why don't you just tell me?"

All the while, David was thinking, *I could just tell her the lessons she learned and the chapter titles. However, I know that learning takes place at a deeper level when people are challenged to discover it within themselves. For Alison to be told and intellectually know the lessons is one thing. For Alison to go within and discover the lessons is learning at an even deeper level.*

As the dinner plates were cleared, David stood up, his six-foot-one frame towering over me, and he said firmly, "No, I am not going to tell you. This is your story. What lessons do you think you learned? In the next five minutes, write down and prioritize the five most important things you have learned." He walked away, and I was floored.

My mind went blank. Then I started to write on the napkin random thoughts, which I then refined and organized. I relaxed into the assignment.

David returned. I had a list of five important lessons. I was excited and amazed and read the list out loud. David smiled knowingly and said, "Exactly! Take a few more minutes and see if the list feels right, and then prioritize however it seems to make sense."

When David sat back down, I shared my handwritten notes. There it was—the outline for the guts of our book (now chapters 5 through 10) had appeared. I still have the napkin.

David knew the outline I was seeking was already there in my conscious and subconscious mind. David knew exactly the process and the lessons he had guided me through during the previous six months. He trusted it was all there. When challenged with an open-ended question, I discovered and experienced that I had the answer all along. Amazing.

Writing my story of discovery and transformation was a big challenge for me. I am a private person and not typically comfortable sharing my innermost feelings with close friends, much less with strangers. Even at this point in my journey, trusting others with my truth is still in its infancy. My grandma's advice to us whenever we were venturing forth into The City was, "Speak to no one—man, woman, nor child." It still resonates in the recesses of my mind.

In fact, the early versions of my story did not include what are now the first three chapters. A probing question from my first editor set up an even bigger challenge for me. He asked, "How can a story of transformation not have a *before* picture and *after* picture of who you used to be compared to who you are now?"

It had been fun and rewarding to share my awakening. It was not nearly as enjoyable to even contemplate writing who I was and how I was perceived since I had relentlessly pursued my personal ambition and the illusion of success for thirty years.

For me, this book is an act of catharsis, courage, and caring. My hope is that by sharing the challenges, the lessons learned, the transformations, and ultimately, the joy of my personal journey, you will find lessons and inspiration for your unique journey.

INTRODUCTION

In everyone's life, at some time, our inner fire goes out.
It is then burst into flame by an encounter
with another human being.
We should all be thankful for
those people who rekindle the inner spirit.

—Albert Schweitzer

I climbed the corporate ladder to heights few women have achieved. Working on Wall Street as managing director at a top-tier global and investment bank, I achieved great financial success and learned a lot about sharp elbows and stress. But September 11, 2001, was a turning point in my life. I had just landed at 8:47 a.m. at LaGuardia and was on my way to a client meeting on the ninety-ninth floor of the World Trade Tower. As I walked outside to meet my limo driver, I could see smoke billowing from one of the World Trade Towers. Minutes later the second terrorist plane hit the other tower, and there was chaos and fear everywhere.

That morning I started on a new life journey. At the time, I did not know what a *"pattern interruption"* was or where I was going, much less anything about personal transformation. What did I need to change? Everything was perfect, right? Wrong.

I was a person who had all the trappings of success—a great career, a seven-figure income, a caring and supportive family—and I was silently, profoundly unhappy.

Nine years later, after changing a lot of my external circumstances—my location, my career, my focus—I realized that little had changed about my inner life. I was very fortunate to start an amazing journey of personal transformation as a client of David Prudhomme, founder of Mederi Wellness and my guide and mind coach. As the great adventurer Albert Schweitzer said, "We should all be thankful for those people who rekindle the inner spirit." I am very grateful, indeed.

What did I learn? What are the lessons for us all? Most importantly, my story shares my experience of *how* I learned these lessons. We all have read many books that instruct us that happiness comes from within. Exactly how does that happen? I share my story and my experiences of *how* I learned these important life lessons.

These are my top six experiential lessons:

1. "The Power to Choose": I learned how to choose my emotions.

2. "Let Go and Take Control": I learned the freedom of letting go.

3. "Forgive and Be Free": I learned how to forgive myself and others.

4. "Release and Rejoice": I learned how to release deep-seated fears.

5. "Look Within and Love Me": I learned what it feels like to unconditionally love yourself and others

6. "I Am Not Special": I learned that I am unique rather than special. We are all the same.

My journey also shares simple, practical lessons for everyone—how to talk to yourself, how you can apply universal truths in your professional career, and how you can prepare your mind for excellence in any sport or endeavor (my example being golf).

By sharing entries from my private journal and by sharing parts of my sessions with David, I hope to convey a sense of the experiential process, what I learned, and more importantly, how I learned universal truths.

I believe you will feel my joy and my pain. I believe you will see how I opened many different doors to my mind, how I explored these deep truths from many vantage points and with different techniques, and how I needed to relearn the lessons many times at deeper and deeper levels.

Are you stuck? Is there something missing in your life? What are you afraid of? What have you not been able to let go of? Who are you intrinsically, aside from your name, family, business, and location? Are you aware of how you talk to yourself in private? How many levels of self-awareness have you discovered? How much more do you want to or think you can discover? Do you know your life's purpose? Are you living your best life?

I will admit that I did not ask myself these questions when I was caught up achieving, running, and climbing the corporate ladder. There just came a point in my life when I finally heard all the wake-up calls that I had received and heretofore ignored. I share when and how I came to know I needed to do something different—and the something different started with looking inside of me. That is when and why I started my sessions with my guide.

What will *you* do?

I share my journey with the purpose to offer you a few ideas, to get you thinking about the next steps for you, and to inspire you with the belief that you can be happy *now*!

The journey continues. It will never end.

Where am I going? Honestly, I am not sure where this new path will take me.

I do know that wherever it takes me, I will walk as a deeply compassionate, content, and happy person.

And now I invite you to start your own unique journey to authentic happiness and to gain a new understanding of yourself and your world through new eyes and new awareness.

PART 1

THREE WAKE-UP CALLS
HELLO ... IS ANYBODY HOME?

CHAPTER 1

September 11 Shatters My Illusion of Success

A contented man is never disappointed.

He who knows when to stop is preserved from peril,

Only thus can you endure long.

—The Tao Te Ching, verse 44

Rendition by Dr. Wayne W. Dyer

It was 9:00 a.m. in New York. I had just landed at LaGuardia after an exhilarating and grueling two-week business trip in Asia. As managing director with a global investment bank, my associates and I had called on some of the largest managers of fixed income portfolios in the world. I was returning to my office on 59th and 5th Ave., the new uptown Wall Street. Still somewhat jet-lagged and forging ahead to prepare for another meeting with an important client at the World Trade Center, I saw an empty hallway and baggage claim area. LaGuardia Airport was eerily quiet.

Where is everyone? I wondered. I heard the scuffle of two people, security personnel, sprinting past me. Where were all the limo drivers with their placards greeting us important people? I walked out the door to look for my driver. There were no horns blaring. It was way too quiet.

Then I saw one of the World Trade Towers burning in the distance. The sight was disconcerting, disorienting, and disturbing. Focused on business as usual, I greeted my driver and asked, "What's going on?" He told me that early reports were that a private plane had crashed into one of the towers. I told my driver, "I need to get to an important meeting in one of the towers." Which tower? Was it the one that was burning? I did not know. I was in routine business mode, yet deep inside, I sensed something was wrong.

As we left La Guardia and were stuck in the traffic jam approaching the Triborough Bridge, we heard on the radio that another plane had just crashed into the second World Trade Tower. In the back seat of the limo, I was in total shock. My throat constricted. My eyes teared up, and I suddenly realized that we, the United States of America, were under attack. We were at war! *I am five hundred miles from home and alone.* Horns were blaring. People on the radio were screaming and I was shaking. I felt totally alone and vulnerable.

As I struggled to make sense of what I was seeing, my driver was very professional and levelheaded, and he tried every way to get into The City. The Triborough Bridge was shut down, and the back way through the Bronx was also blocked. Manhattan was on lockdown. Emotions were running high. Two big truck drivers were out of their cabs, screaming at the top of their deep voices. Their trucks had hit each other in the middle of an intersection. The drivers were angry and scared.

I was frightened—eyes wide open and seeing nothing and not believing what I was seeing. "Please just get me out of here!" was my prayer. It was everything I could do to contain my trembling and speak in full sentences. It took every ounce of energy to stay in control on the outside, while I felt the world crumbling around me.

Then it came to me. Aunt Mary would save me.

I asked my driver if it were possible to take me to Aunt Mary's home, which was two hours north of The City in the small town of Craryville. To my relief and amazement, he agreed. Then I discovered I had left my cell phone in my car in the Cleveland airport. It must have been the jet lag as my cell phone was never off my person. Coincidence? My driver again was a lifesaver. I managed to make one call out to Aunt Mary. I wanted to let her know I was safe and that I was coming to her house. Then all the lines were jammed. No cell phone communication was possible.

As we headed north, we listened to the live radio coverage of the disaster. The screams and the chaos down at the towers were bone-chilling and penetrating, even from the security of the limo. The radio reporters were bringing the tragedy into the car. It was surreal. I was looking out the window of the limo at a beautiful clear blue sky with hints of autumn in the leaves just starting to turn color. Nature was beautiful that day, which was in stark contrast to the death and destruction I was hearing and escaping.

I had flown to NYC to meet with one of our clients on the ninety-ninth floor of the second World Trade Tower. The timing was strangely miraculous. I could have been there—there but for the grace of God. The tears were streaming down my face. I was so scared and so thankful for my own safety. I could not even begin to imagine the horror and the heartbreak of the people in the towers and their families.

I looked out the rearview window and saw the thick plumes of black smoke turn white, reaching high into the sky. The radio reported that the World Trade Towers were collapsing—first one and then the other. As the towers came down, the smoke turned white, and I turned white. "All those poor innocent souls, may they rest in peace," I silently prayed. Black smoke turned to white. The imagery was powerful.

I said another silent prayer and got shivers. Tears streamed down my cheeks. I was praying over and over, "Our Father who art in heaven ..." On the radio's live coverage, the screams were horrific, the chaos unimaginable. I was safe, and I did not feel safe. I could not stop shaking.

***

That day I stayed with my Aunt Mary. I was glued to the TV's nonstop coverage. I was following all the reports and seeing the horrifying videos over and over. I went through the motions. From Aunt Mary's rotary landline, I checked in with my husband, Doug, who had been fielding calls of concern all day. He did not know of the events until a friend called him and he turned on the TV. Aunt Mary shortly thereafter called him and told him I was coming to her home. I checked on my closest associates. All were safe.

By the next day, Wednesday, I was ready to plan the logistics to return home and to work. The airports were closed until further notice. My mind was spinning. *What should I do? Should I rent a car and drive fifteen hours to Ohio or take the train back to NYC? What can I do? What did I want to do?*

I was shaken to the core. I could not stop crying. My mind was racing. And I knew instinctively that it was not the time to make any big life decisions. I just needed to focus on the next steps, putting one foot in front of the other. I prayed, "Please, Lord, deliver me from this nightmare!" It felt like I was on my own. I decided to take the first flight out of Albany when the airports reopened and to return to Ohio.

***

There I was in a bucolic upstate New York setting of rolling hills. I was taking walks and watching the birds. The deer came down to feed in the evening. The TV was on, and reality intruded with constant replays of the World Trade Towers collapsing. I was on the phone to the office every hour, checking on associates and learning who had been lost. To this day, the surreal contrast of the idyllic setting with the reality of the news from the TV and phone remains the most powerful image in my memory. My mind and emotions were on overdrive.

At that point, I thought it was all about my intellect. My brain had gotten me here. What came to my mind? I had been working in New York City with people, some of whom I did not like and many who did not like me. All of the stress came to the forefront—the commuting weekly, the working with all the *sharp elbows*, which is the modus operandi of many on the Street, the travail of working seventy-plus hours a week, building two new strategy groups from scratch on a shoestring budget, and the high demands and expectations.

What was I really doing? What did I want? What were my priorities? What did I need to change in my life? What was my plan?

For more than ten years, I had been racking up frequent flier miles, first in the United States and then with international travel, making calls

7

with our sales people on major global investors in London and Paris. I had been invited to speak at an international conference on credit derivatives with more than a thousand attendees. The topic involved the research on credit defaults in the high-yield market, which utilized a third-party technology on the probability of default at the company level. Heady stuff. I had made three trips to Asia to meet with global fixed-income investors in Hong Kong, China, Indonesia, Singapore and South Korea. My understanding of the global markets and the level of sophistication of global investors had been growing exponentially.

With the support of my boss and with the support of all the fixed-income research analysts, some of whom reported directly to me and many of whom were in specialized teams, we had produced a quarterly credit strategy compendium that covered our strategic asset allocation recommendations and detailed company-specific relative value trade recommendations. This was a first-class research product, and it positioned the firm to rank with the top sell-side securities firms. I add this detail to acknowledge the wonderful contributions of the terrifically smart and talented analysts I had the pleasure of working with. I also want to acknowledge how much I grew and learned professionally from this experience.

Did I love this life on Wall Street and international travel? Hmm. Not really. I was never home. I never had time to breathe. Did I love who I had become? Hmm. Who was I? Who had I become? Yes, the money was nice. The accoutrements of the lifestyle were awesome and beyond my wildest expectations. Was this really who I was?

What were my feelings? As I processed all these thoughts, I felt like a zombie. Either I couldn't feel anything, or I was so overwhelmed with emotions that had been buried deep within that I could not stop crying.

So what was I feeling? After the initial shock on the morning of 9/11, the bone penetrating fear subsided. I knew I was safe. I felt very alone. I was disconnected from everyone and everything I really loved, including myself. I was desolate. The emptiness inside of me was vast. I did not feel successful. I just felt driven—by myself and by others' expectations for me to do even more.

In the great Catholic tradition, I have a confession. What were my prayers? I was praying nonstop my "Hail Mary," my "Our Father." The prayers were rote, a crutch. I was not a person of faith at this point in my journey.

On reflection, there are so many reasons why I felt empty. I was chasing ambition and money. I was always on the go, headed to the next event and focused on the next deadline. I was controlling my emotions, which meant that I was suppressing and denying my emotions of resentment, anger, and self-pity. I had no faith, no soul, not a glimmer of spirituality.

My life had spiraled out of control, totally out of my control. That week in the safety and serenity of upstate New York, I realized that I did not want to go back to work in New York City.

I was not afraid of the terrorists. I just felt so totally, so terribly alone. More importantly, I just knew in my gut that I was not living a life that was true to me.

***

During the next six months, I decided it was time to start to reclaim control of my life, to shift away from my Wall Street ambitions, and to put family first. It was not all about fame and fortune. This was my life, and I wanted to take control.

To say this decision was not easy is an understatement of enormous proportions. What was I giving up? Money? Yes. It was a very scary thought.

And yet I knew in my heart it was time for me to decide what was right for me. The trauma was so deep that I simply had to listen to my inner voice. At the time I had never heard of the term *pattern interruption*, which we will discuss later. I had not learned to listen to my intuition and my heart. I had no perspective or understanding that I was at a major turning point. I was simply doing what I knew I needed to do to survive. Sometimes we learn the lessons by looking through the rearview mirror.

Over the next several months, I decided to set in motion a careful plan to put my family first and to bring my professional life into the same geographic plane as my personal life. The timing was fortunate for me. There was a reorganization in the works, and I happened to qualify for early retirement. (No coincidences in life, right? Everything happens for a reason.) My managers were supportive and appreciative of the credit strategy research initiative I had helped build.

I left the bank on good terms, and I left the life, my career that I had known for more than twenty-five years. It was a gut-wrenching decision.

I just pulled the rip cord.

CHAPTER 2
Ambition Stirs

It is ordained that to the ambitious,
who derive no satisfaction from the gifts of life
and the beauty of the world,
life shall be a cause of suffering, and
they shall possess neither the profit
nor the beauty of the world.

—Leonardo da Vinci

At the outset, my intent was to share the story about my journey from Wall Street and my focus on ambition and money and reveal how I came home to the real me. My only goal was to share my experience of the process of going deeply within, guided by David Prudhomme and his proprietary framework, The Best Me NOW! If somehow this book helps one person or one thousand people discover the happiness within themselves, I will be overjoyed.

My first editor challenged me, "How can a story of transformation not have a *before* and *after* picture?" In other words, it may be fun to write about how I have changed, but readers still needed to know where I came from.

It hurt to write this chapter. I was shedding my armor and revealing where I came from, how I came to be perceived, and how I did not listen to my inner voice for most of my career.

***

When I left Ohio State with an MA in economics, only a dissertation short of a PhD, all I knew was that I did not want to teach and write esoteric articles. I wanted to get out into the real world and see what the practical world of business was all about.

Ambition stirred. Oh, yeah, I also got married and left two other boyfriends behind.

I started my professional career in a regional bank in Kentucky as a filing clerk. However, I never accepted that as my reality, much less the extent of my job and what I could do. I was also an instructor at a local community college, teaching macroeconomics, microeconomics, and statistics. The bank, which was starting to form a research group to support the portfolio managers in the trust department, offered me a position. Management did not believe they needed an economist. They had just let a consulting agreement lapse with an economist who was too boring and irrelevant. They were hiring MBAs for the new research department, so I was both overqualified and underqualified. Sound familiar?

With unbounded optimism ... or unbridled ego and arrogance, I snapped at the opportunity to work as an assistant in the research department—as a clerk.

I filed papers for about six months, finished teaching my courses at the local community college, and then wangled a chance to be the bank stock analyst. I knew about interest rate cycles, sort of. I did not know how to read a balance sheet or income statement. I had never taken even one accounting course. With fervor and drive, I went to *school*. The markets were my education. The stock market made me smart by showing me the practical application of all my book learning. I was learning so much and having a blast.

I worked hard, harder than all the boys. I earned my CFA, the certification of Chartered Financial Analyst. At the time, that certification required passing tests in seven disciplines, including ethics, quantitative methods, economics, corporate finance, financial reporting and analysis, security analysis, and portfolio management at three successively higher levels over a minimum of five years in the industry. The CFA is a prestigious certification that all the up-and-coming Wall Street analysts were earning.

I also made sure I met the *right* people and cultivated the *right* business associates. I was intent on making it in a man's world. I was a sought-after *brain*, an original thinker.

I got a taste of how smart I was, how good I was, and what a standout woman I could be in the financial world. I never looked back—at least not until recently.

As I moved into the ambition and career achievement phase of my life, I left behind many of the values with which I had been raised. My middle-class upbringing in a strict Scotch-Irish Catholic family on Long Island emphasized family, faith, humility, frugality, sports, work ethic, and humanitarianism. Those values were overshadowed by my pursuit of what I had never had, namely freedom and money.

I was very fortunate to have important senior male mentors early on in my career. I learned from them all, and ultimately, I left them all ... in my career pursuit of my own bigger opportunities, my ambitions.

I was also fortunate to cross paths with many intelligent, professional women. One woman in particular was a kindred spirit. She was very bright, with a brilliant smile and acerbic wit. These special bonds and friendships helped sustain me and helped me keep my sense of humor and laugh at the foolishness of all the posturing and the politics.

In the course of moving from Louisville to Washington, DC, to Chicago, I had two major setbacks. The last move entailed a major salary cut and a job with people who made me wail, "What have I done?" The details are less important than the lessons I took from them. I learned how to fight in the corporate world. I resolved not to be "put in my place." I would prevail. I did prevail.

I had wonderful opportunities over eleven different assignments—both staff and line assignments—at progressively higher levels. The titles and bonuses were whetting my appetite and stroking my ego. I survived the failure of Continental Bank, several management restructurings, and two major acquisitions.

I learned early and quickly to always look ahead to my next opportunity, to *be* at the next level. Then the promotions naturally followed.

I did not come from money. My dad was disdainful of money and heritage or inheritance. "Why should you care?" he would ask. I was brought up to actually brush aside any perception of people's money, and I was taught not to want money. Then in banking I learned money was the measuring stick. I learned to negotiate, to press to be paid like my peers, to be paid like the men.

As it happened, I was almost always offered a position previously held by a man. The new responsibility brought a better salary for me and less compensation than the man had earned. I was moving up, and the person I replaced was moving out and/or moving on. My talent was to bring a new look, a new way of doing things. That was my forte. Guess what? When it was my turn to move on, a man almost always replaced me. These experiences fueled my determination and probably my ego and resentment too.

I had a knack for making money. My husband and I played the real estate market right for thirty years. We played the interest rate cycle right. I earned options in the upswing of the stock market. I ended up making six figures on base salary and seven figures on options, all lucky on the timing. I even cashed in my options at the right time.

I was fortunate to be smart and lucky. I was only peripherally aware that I threatened insecure men, and often I was not even cognizant of their insecurity. Some people were jealous, and my arrogance was thinly concealed. What did I care what other people thought?

I moved from the banking side to the securities side of the business as soon as deregulation opened up that area to BankAmerica. I knew that was where the money was. I also liked the markets. I have always said, "The markets make you smart." I was always looking to learn and achieve, always pressing forward, always striving.

Why? What was driving me to achieve, to chase all my illusions of success? Here's one answer, of which I am not very proud. *Because I could.* My training, intellectual prowess, and distinctive ability to see patterns and connections allowed me to be a standout performer. It was pride and ego.

What were the other driving forces? At the time, I did not even give it a passing thought. As I walk my journey and now have an opportunity to honestly reflect, the answer probably lies in my deep-seated emotions of anger, resentment, and fear, feeling as if I needed to be better in order to be good enough.

***

So who had I become? Culling from various employee feedback surveys, I gleaned a few insights from friends who knew me then. Soft on the outside, steel on the inside. So quick, so intuitive that some believed I had a hidden agenda. I could be seen as Machiavellian. Good on tasks and deadlines, not so good on trust and relationships. Not very good at delegating. Good at coaching some people, the ones who were bright and talented. Abrasive, not user-friendly, changeable, demanding, deliberate, dogmatic, methodical, opinionated. Analytical, decisive, dependable, detached, determined, energetic, independent, initiating, reflective, self-confident.

On my leadership style, people wanted me to be more appreciative, compromising, considerate, delegating, methodical, patient, permissive, and trusting.

On my interpersonal style, people wanted me to be less abrasive, blunt, dogmatic, impatient, and manipulating. There is a saying that some people "do not suffer fools gladly." At the time, I would have taken that as a compliment. As I have learned, there is also a significant amount of arrogance and judgment in that belief.

Indeed, I learned that I tested more than three standard deviations outside the norm on "thinking outside of the box." People often couldn't quite follow my thinking. I was not very self-aware.

Given this feedback, how did I get to where I was? I must have been doing *something* right. Right? Sure, I was a tenacious, exceptional, smart, results-oriented professional and a woman in a man's world.

I was able to create new processes and policies, effect organizational change, and get results. Every new position was an invitation and an opportunity to effect change. That was one of my strengths. I was really never given a mandate. My ability to think three standard deviations outside of the box was a core strength I brought to the mission and to the assignment at hand.

When I moved over to the "sell side" and to the Wall Street securities side of the business, most of my managers only valued results. So much for all the historical feedback!

Or as Shakespeare so eloquently phrased it, "I come to bury Caesar, not to praise him."

***

As I was climbing the corporate ladder of promotions, titles, and bonuses, I got a few wake-up calls. As a result, I started to pay a little more attention to family and to my relationships with friends.

I lost my brother Ricky to a brain tumor the year he was to turn thirty years old. Ricky had a brain tumor removed when he was in high school. I was only told after the fact. Ten years later we learned there was a second tumor. Mom, Dad, and I flew out to be with Ricky and his wife for his surgery. The surgery was a success.

About one month later, we learned there was a third tumor at the base of Ricky's brain, and it was inoperable. It was only a matter of time. It was devastating to our family, to my Mom most of all. For years and years and years, I could not talk about Ricky without huge emotions welling up and uncontrollable tears. Repressed emotions have a way of coming out.

Ricky was brilliant. He aspired to be an author, working in the summers in West Yellowstone and writing in the winters. He had a dream. His dream was cut short. He was far too young. I did not know how to let him go. Letting go is one of the most important lessons I have since learned. I now love to talk about Ricky, his life in Yellowstone Park, his dreams of writing novels in the Yellowstone winters, and his beautiful soul. It is now my goal to publish his nonfiction short stories in his honor.

We laid Ricky to rest and to peace in a simple pine casket in the cemetery woods outside of West Yellowstone in late May. I placed a handpicked bouquet of beautiful forget-me-nots at the gravesite. To me they are forever Ricky's flower.

From that day forward, I spoke to Mom and Dad every week.

Several years later my Grandma, my personal hero, passed away. Grandma had raised seven children through the Great Depression, worked at Macy's on 34th Street in New York City, and scrubbed floors at St. Michael's at night to keep the family together. Her unbounded love, sense of humor, and awe of nature have stayed with me always.

Aunt Mary, the oldest child of the seven on my Mother's side of the family, was destined to be Grandma's caregiver, foreshadowing future events. My Aunt Mary cared for Grandma every day for nine years until Grandma succumbed to the progressive effects of dementia and required the 24-7 care of a nursing home.

Then my Mom passed away very suddenly. One day she was waving good-bye to me after a visit. Two days later she passed in her sleep without warning.

From that day on, I spoke with Mary every Saturday, taking the place of my mother's weekly call to her. I spoke with my Dad every Sunday morning without fail.

There were responsibilities on my husband's side of the family as well. We had become the primary caregivers for both his aunt and his mother. It seemed every year we were moving one or both of them and trying to figure out the logistics from long distance.

The yellow lights were flashing. Did I stop doing what I was doing? No, I had never known or dreamed of such financial freedom. I bought what I wanted when I wanted. We enjoyed eating out and expanding our culinary tastes. It was exhilarating to expand my borders and experiences. I was determined I could and would succeed in the world of banking, a man's world.

Did I understand the toll my career and my ambition were taking on me mentally, physically, and emotionally? No.

Hello. Is Anybody Home?

Did I tap on the brakes and make a few adjustments? Yes. I started doing a much better job of staying connected with family and nurturing certain relationships.

As my Dad used to say, "The light was only pink." That was exactly my mentality toward the flashing yellow caution lights—a shrug of my shoulders and a laugh. I was truly oblivious to what was really going on in my life. I pushed on.

Then in the course of one year, specifically 1998, my world was rocked. Guess what? I stalwartly soldiered on.

My Dad called just before Christmas to say he had been diagnosed with lung cancer. After many tests the doctors told us he likely had less than a year to live.

Our dog, Chip, was diagnosed with bone cancer on his leg. Bone cancer can be horribly painful. We tried surgery. It was only forestalling the inevitable.

My husband lost his company because of a combination of strategic and personality differences between Doug and his investors/board members.

Bank of America, my employer, was acquired by NationsBank, and my job was on the line. I was offered an opportunity to head up a new unit, Credit Strategy Research, which required a move or a commute to New York City.

In my heart I was crying. My Dad, my husband, our chocolate Lab—so many looming issues and losses. The pain was awful. And I was very experienced at burying my emotions. On the outside, I soldiered on in full armor. What was my response? Put the pedal to the metal. There were so many people who depended on me.

***

I am reminded of the time in Louisville, Kentucky, when I was teaching at a community college and had to park in a small cramped parking lot under the overpass of a major highway. I was still learning to drive my husband's '65 Chevy, a stick shift. I was stuck between another car and a pillar. I maneuvered, shifted, and maneuvered. I was stuck. What could I do? What did I do? Trapped and frightened, I pressed the gas pedal, trashed the side of the car on the concrete pillar, and escaped! Nothing could stop me, not even a concrete pillar.

In 1998, I accepted the position in New York City and started my weekly commute.

There is a prophetic story from that year. My first wake-up call from that year of turmoil was the day my Dad passed on September 11, 1998. My next major wake-up call was exactly three years later on September 11, 2001, the day of the terrorist attack on the World Trade Centers. There are no coincidences.

I spent much of that year of Dad's illness traveling to upstate New York, spending a week and then another week and then another week, all the while in the throes of merger issues. I was *negotiating* the future structure of the new research organization and the opportunities and fates of the people who worked for me. I put *negotiating* in italics because it was only an illusion. I had no control.

I had always been very close to my Dad. I had thought of Dad as my biggest supporter, my coach. Mom had sometimes felt like my biggest critic. Dad taught me to play tennis and golf. He watched every sporting event on TV, and I relished the time we spent together, absorbed in the games and competition.

Of the four children still living, I was the one who wrote and delivered the graveside eulogy for Dad (Theodore or Ted or Doc). Here is an excerpt:

> Dad, we loved you for all you taught us, for how deeply
> you loved and cared for Mom and all of us. And for
> who you are—a man who was honest as the day is long;
> a man of keen intelligence; a man who valued common
> sense above all; a man with deep convictions and who
> was not judgmental; a man who treated all people as
> individuals, rejecting stereotypes; and most of all, a
> man with a great sense of humor.
> I suppose coming from a family where your father and
> his brothers had nicknames of Dino, Fifo, and Nino,
> you came by your unique sense of humor honestly. You
> always believed—and taught us—that being different
> was good. It really just meant being yourself and not
> taking yourself too seriously.
> Our memory bank is rich, thanks to you, Dad. This walk
> with you down memory lane would not be complete if
> we didn't talk some more about sports. Dad's love for
> sports was integral to his values—to do your best and
> have some fun. It was integral to your way of caring for
> each of us. If it was a sport, we played it. We watched
> it. We talked about it with you. Roller skating, football,
> baseball, tennis, ice skating, hockey, stickball, polo, cards,

billiards, Ping-Pong, sledding, bowling—the list goes on and on. And of course, golf. Dad had a one-liner for sports … and for life too. "Don't think. Just hit the ball." Dad, we all treasure your advice. We will miss you deeply, and we know that Mom and you are always with us in our hearts. We love you, Dad.

—The Lanza Family

The day after I came home from the funeral, I boarded a plane for San Francisco for an important business conference. I was numb.

That week I started to talk to my brother every Sunday morning, taking the place of my weekly talk with Dad.

What was I thinking? It was survival, pushing through and burying family and personal problems. I was focused on the financial rewards, ambition, and the trappings of success.

I was not thinking. I was just trying very hard to survive and take care of everyone. We moved from Chicago to Port Clinton so my husband could care for his Mom. I started my weekly commute to New York City.

The more revealing question is as follows: What was I feeling? If asked, "How are you feeling?" I would always answer, "Just fine!" It is the classic cultural lie.

In hindsight, what was I feeling? I can see some patterns in my life, my behavior, and my feelings.

For instance, enough was never enough. I was being challenged by my bosses to do more with almost no budget. No matter how well my group performed and how much we contributed to building high-level strategic relationships with clients, there was always some blowup in the markets, in the industry, or in another department of the bank. The bonus pool was cut. This was certainly not a unique experience to my group and me. It was just a fact of life in the banking industry at the time.

In addition, there was self-doubt. I was not good enough. As far as I had climbed on the ladder of titles, financial rewards, bonuses, and stock options, I still felt a need to prove myself. I had my to-do lists every morning and updated them every evening. Could I really make it on Wall Street? Could I live up to my expectations, and could I compete with the best on the Street?

When I came home, I needed to be the *good wife*, host gatherings of friends, feed the birds, and also walk and connect with our chocolate lab, Zacharia. In truth, I wanted to prove I could do it all. I was continuously running, and I was exhausted.

Was I depressed? *Absolutely not!* I thought. I had a great career. I was very well compensated. The international travel was exciting, and I was seeing places I had only dreamed of ever seeing—London, Paris, Thailand, Hong Kong, the Great Wall of China. I was fortunate to be able to come home to family and friends and a big lake house.

Yet I had every reason to be depressed. I had lost my brother, my mother, and my father. I was detached and unaware. I was so wrapped up in the doing and the achieving that I never gave much thought to myself. I really did not know who I was and where I was going.

In retrospect, I was driven and in denial. I was deeply sad.

CHAPTER 3
Same Old Gravy, Just Warmed Over

*Insanity: doing the same thing
over and over again and
expecting different results.*

—Albert Einstein

In 2002, I had come home to Doug and Ohio—except I had come home to a place where I had never lived and where I had no close friends. In my career, every time I had taken a new assignment, I had the philosophy that I was starting from square one with both the new people and with what needed to be done. Deep breath. One more time.

I put together a plan to do consulting and build a portfolio of board memberships. As a board member, my financial and strategic planning expertise has value. I also wanted to find opportunities to give back, so I was looking for the right fit with both nonprofit boards and corporate boards.

I was committed to make the time to really learn the game of golf and hone my skills.

I had changed many things but all on the outside.

I had changed my location and home. No more commuting every week. However, I was traveling all over the state, networking in the Port Clinton area, Toledo, Cleveland, and Columbus. I was also going back to Chicago and New York and Washington, DC, to renew old contacts. I was flying to Albany to look in on Aunt Mary.

I had changed my career focus to be a consultant and a professional board member. I took one whole month to decompress and then was back hard at it. (Wow, one whole month? Imagine that extravagance!) I created an LLC, filled my calendar with meetings, took on a major consulting engagement, attended meetings, networked, networked, and networked nonstop. I joined the National Association of Corporate Directors to hone my knowledge of the fiduciary responsibilities of board members. I kept up my membership in the CFA Institute and joined the local chapter, the Cleveland Society of Financial Analysts. I became a founding member of In Counsel With Women, an organization for the top hundred women in northeast Ohio. I was busier than ever.

I also scheduled in some time for myself, enjoying golf and having some time for fun. I took golf lessons, joined a local women's golf league, and was focused on getting better and better. I gradually and impatiently brought my handicap down from thirty-six ... to thirty-two ... to twenty-six ... to twenty-two. More lessons, more tournaments. I am a little competitive. You think?

I was enjoying life more and feeling more fulfilled. My service on the Board of United Way of Greater Toledo (UWGT) and Advisory Board of the Trust for Public Land (Ohio office) was wonderful. I had an opportunity to lead a national search for a new CEO of UWGT. I was then elected to serve as the next Chair of the Board of Trustees for UWGT. I was relishing the opportunity to start to introduce stronger governance practices to this organization, which did wonderful work in Lucas, Wood, and Ottawa counties. The new CEO was bringing many changes to the organization, and I worked to revitalize the board to support him and the mission work of United Way of Greater Toledo.

In working with The Trust for Public Land, I was able to interest them in a very complex conservation project to protect fourteen acres on the shore of Lake Erie in downtown Port Clinton. After a long, drawn-out three-year process, the deal closed, and the city of Port Clinton had a new park and an opportunity to restore wetlands and build a trail for people to enjoy nature. Bravo! "If not for you" is the well-deserved brand for The Trust for Public Land.

The Governor of Ohio also appointed me to a reconstituted Board of Directors of the Ohio Bureau of Workers Compensation. I was one of two investment professionals on the board. Together we led a comprehensive review and restructuring of the $19 billion investment portfolio. This was the most amazing board experience for me. The new Chairman of the Board set a terrifically open and respectful tone and environment for all the newly appointed board members. In addition, after the scandal and years of inattention to best practices, the board had a very serious challenge to work with the new Administrator to review and overhaul policies and to institute good governance practices.

Importantly, I also decided to join a local church. My faith was nascent, a small step from nonexistent. I felt that guardian angels had been watching over me, protecting me through my weekly commute, global travels, and 9/11. As I attended church on a somewhat irregular basis, I started to feel the presence of the Holy Spirit. Next thing I knew, I was elected an Elder and asked to chair the Financial Stewardship Committee.

Golf had become a passion. I was playing more, learning more, and even winning a few tournaments. I was using my prowess and achievement as a way to start to build relationships in a new community. That's what high achievers in business did, right? Indeed, people applaud winners. That is endemic to our culture. And in retrospect, there is a lot of ego, however well camouflaged. Please don't misunderstand me. I continue to love to play golf. I relish in competition that brings out the best in me and in others. And I had yet to learn at that point that winning a trophy is a passing glory and it has very little to do with finding happiness.

I had changed many things, and I had not changed myself. There were a lot of really good new things happening in my life on the surface. And yet I hadn't changed my behaviors. Had I changed my modus operandi, the traits that had made me successful for thirty years? Not really.

I would simply observe that I was still driven and in denial. Underneath, I was still stressed and exhausted. This goes a long way in explaining why I was so ill-prepared to handle the life challenges that were coming.

***

And so I arrive at another personal life crisis in 2009.

I now see this series of events as another wake-up call. How many wake-up calls have you had? How many wake-up calls have you ignored?

This was my third wake-up call, and it was a call to action, although I did not know it at the time. I guess I must have been deeply asleep and intensely unaware.

In the summer of 2009, I was in the parking lot on the phone with Aunt Mary, and I was about to join my husband, Doug, for a relaxing dinner after a round of golf. A waitress came running out of the restaurant toward me. Her hands were in the air, and she was screaming, "He's down!" In that instant I thought my husband was dead.

When I entered the restaurant, I was dazed and in shock. Doug was just getting up. I was, of course, relieved, yet the fear was still very much inside me. It turned out Doug had inexplicably blacked out. Did he have a stroke or a heart attack? Why was his ankle all swollen? We called EMS. After a weekend of tests, there was still no explanation for the blackout. Surgery was required for his broken ankle, which involved inserting seven pins.

After the surgery the prognosis was good. Doug was confined to bed for two weeks. Full recovery took at least six weeks. I was his nurse. He was confined to the bedroom on the second floor. I took up breakfast, lunch, and dinner and provided all the care and support he needed.

On its own, this does not sound so tough. And after all, he was very lucky. I was so thankful he was alive.

Then my dear Aunt Mary fell and was rushed to the hospital. Mary had broken her neck, and there was internal bleeding. After the ambulance trip to the local hospital, we were transported by EMS for treatment by specialists in Toledo. This happened just two weeks to the day after Doug's fall.

***

Allow me to set the stage. For the two months prior to both these accidents, my personal life had already been chaotic.

Mary was my *other mother*. We had become very close, and we had a lot in common. For more than ten years, since my mother Eileen's passing, I talked with Mary every Saturday morning. I traveled to see her every year ... and then twice a year ... and then three times a year ... and then every other month. Along the way I made a sacred promise to my Uncle Bill, Mary's only surviving sibling, that I would always take care of Mary. Mary was a retired banker. She had a very successful career in New York City. She and her husband never had children, and we both liked things to be *just so*. Mary was beautiful, Katherine Hepburn-like beautiful.

For years I had wanted Mary close to me so I could take care of her, and she had refused because she did not want to be a burden to me. As the independent person that she had always been, she decided to sell her house up in the beautiful hills of upstate New York and move to an independent living complex outside of Albany. I managed all of her moves and the sale of the house, staying weeks and then a month to get her resituated and making sure everything was *just so*.

Then her friends began telling me she needed to be "closer to family." That was code that they were very concerned. Mary's dementia was progressing. I used all my organizational skills to make the move happen. I researched several options and found a suitable retirement complex ten minutes from my house. I lined up a new lease on a nice condo. I lined up packers and movers. One day I swooped in for a visit. Mary agreed it was time to move. I had everything staged. The very next day we said good-bye to her friends. That same day my husband arrived after he made the thirteen-hour trip by car. Doug's assignment was to pick up Mary's cat, Boy, and take the few essentials I had packed for Mary to move from New York to Ohio. The next day Mary and I boarded a flight to Cleveland and traveled to our lake house. That same day the packers arrived, and for the next three days, they packed up everything in the apartment in New York. There was a lot of stuff. Nothing was sorted out. I was just glad a friend made sure they didn't pack up the garbage.

In Ohio, Mary was living with us. Mary woke up one morning, and she said, "I can't live here with you." I knew Mary did not want to be a burden and very much needed to have her independence, so I put the next phase into action. The moving van arrived from New York, and for five days straight, I unpacked and arranged a new apartment to look almost exactly like her old apartment. One Friday, we took Mary for a drive and opened the door to her new apartment. Mary was overjoyed. She said, "This looks just like home!" After a frenetic three weeks of planning and moving, Mary was in Ohio, and things were falling into place.

However, Mary was really disoriented, and understandably so. I was seeing the truth about how her dementia had progressed. I was with Mary every day, and pretty much every day was a new mini crisis. She didn't know how to use the phone or the microwave. Mary was wandering outside in the parking lot.

Two weeks after I moved Mary into her new apartment, my husband Doug fell. Two weeks after that crisis, Mary fell.

So there I was, in the hospital with Mary. It was 2:00 a.m. For hours she had been crying out, "Alison, don't leave me!" and I was at her side. Mary's second vertebra and her pelvis were both fractured. The good news was that the internal bleeding had stopped. Mary's neck was stable now, and she had been sedated. We had a fabulous doctor who understood the treatment of this type of injury in older people when their skulls are very thin. He fit her with a collar brace, not a head brace that screws into the skull.

For me, this was a living nightmare. I had just moved Mary to be with me after she had put it off for years and years. Now she had a broken neck. Oh, my God, what had I done? Lord, have mercy.

Mary left the hospital, and after two and a half months in a rehabilitation facility, she made a miraculous recovery. However, the events had accelerated her dementia and required a move into an assisted living apartment. In the space of four months, Mary had moved from one apartment in upstate New York into another apartment in Ohio into a rehab facility and then into an assisted living apartment. That's a lot of moves for anyone. Mary was understandably confused. Mary was amazing in her resilience and her loving-kindness. All this while, my good neighbor Bob was helping me by taking care of Mary's cat, Boy. We were doing everything possible to see Mary reunited with Boy when she moved into her new assisted living apartment. The healing power of love and pets is very real.

***

As events had unfolded in the summer of 2009, I became a full-time caregiver. I was totally exhausted and humbled. All these events were out of my control. All my talents, my expertise, and my resources could not help me shape or control the situation.

Our devoted Zacharia, our ten-year-old, 115-pound chocolate lab, was suffering from crippling arthritis, and then he developed epileptic seizures. The doctors, the nurses, the aides, and now my vet had become my daily companions. They were all wonderful.

My friends told me that nothing had better happen to me. I needed to take care of myself because everyone was depending on me. Exactly how was I supposed to take care of myself with so many demands on my time and when my life was so totally out of control?

The real issue was that I had tried very hard to stay in control and that my life was once again out of control. I had pushed all my real emotions deep below the surface. I was running on empty. I was mired in self-pity. I was still in denial and still driven.

And I felt guilty. Surely, other people had much larger personal tragedies in their lives. How was it that I could not handle this situation better? Surely, super-successful Alison should be able to take all these events in stride. Right? Well, I was not feeling very successful. I felt guilty because I had every reason to feel happy.

This was a moment of truth. Fast-forward to the spring of 2010. We all made it to the next year. My husband, Doug, was fully recovered and doing great. Aunt Mary was out of rehab and in a beautiful assisted living apartment with her faithful cat, Boy. I was sitting at my kitchen table, alone, and I thought to myself, *Be honest.* I was not happy. I needed help. But from where?

PART 2

OPENING NEW DOORS OF MY MIND

CHAPTER 4
I Choose One Day in May

Change is a constant. Growth is a choice.

—David S. Prudhomme

My journey started at noon on May 3, 2010, and I did not even know it at the time.

My journey—a journey from Wall Street ambition and the illusion of success to happiness and unconditional love of myself—is a personal account that's told from my heart, one of discovery, awareness, and experiential learning. The journey is a constant cycle with many iterations and dimensions and settings of discovery, awareness, and understanding, all of which lead to learning through experiencing the lesson. The process is more than simply reading, thinking, following lists, and checking boxes.

In this sense, walking a labyrinth is a wonderful metaphor for my journey, for all of our journeys through life. Walking a labyrinth is a walking meditation, and you experience the journey. Everyone's journey is unique. Everyone's experience in walking a labyrinth is different, and it may be different every time you walk the labyrinth. There is an endless stream of new things to learn and experience in the cycle of life.

As I use the term, experiential learning means learning by doing and integrates the knowledge and emotions contained in both the conscious and subconscious minds, which is incredibly important. Consider the following quotation that describes the process of experiential learning:

> *Learning is finding out what you already know.*
> *Doing is demonstrating you know it.*
> *Teaching is reminding others that they know*
> *just as well as you.*
> *You are all learners, doers, teachers.*

> —Richard Bach, from *Illusions: The*
> *Adventures of a Reluctant Messiah; The*
> *Messiah's Handbook: Reminders for the*
> *Advanced Soul*

I chose one day in May 2010, May 3 to be exact, to consult on stress and weight loss with David S. Prudhomme, founder of Mederi Wellness. Dare I say it out loud? I was desperate.

I had successfully transitioned from an amazingly lucrative career on Wall Street to a productive and fulfilling role as an active board member on five boards.

And I was not happy. Hold on a minute. I had every reason to be happy. I had substantial financial resources, a beautiful lake house, a wonderful husband, a devoted chocolate Lab, and a loving family, especially my other mother, my dear aunt Mary.

In the last chapter, "Same Old Gravy, Just Warmed Over," I was dealing with a couple of family health crises and had become a full-time caregiver. My family, the reason I came home from Wall Street, survived the trials of 2009. All was good, and I was a mess. I had gained weight. I was drinking too much, and I was not able to control my stress. I was a saint and a sinner. I was full of self-pity. I was desperate, and nobody really knew except me because I had learned how to control my public persona.

I told no one that I had made an appointment to see David Prudhomme. I was too proud. I was afraid. What would people think? What would David see in me? I already knew the worst. I was desperate. I did not like myself.

When we met, I came dressed in my corporate suit, my armor, prepared for battle, with a list of twenty-plus questions. I interviewed him! Actually, I interrogated him. On reflection, perhaps there was a little of my New York attitude and arrogance in my approach. David simply smiled and relaxed, answered my probing questions and we talked for more than an hour as he shared his philosophy and understanding of the mind and human behavior. Then, I was satisfied that I knew him and was willing to proceed with two hypnosis sessions on stress and weight loss. After all, my mind was my livelihood. I would not entrust my mind to just anyone.

And so my journey began.

When I started, I did not know where I was going. I did not have a plan, and yet I had a reputation as a very planful person in my professional life.

Little did I know at the time that David Prudhomme had a program, The Best Me NOW!, a process that he would shape and tailor to my unique situation.

From my perspective it was one step at a time, and it just flowed. When I allowed it to flow and did not force it, it took time, and it just happened. It was easy. It was natural. It was wonderful beyond words.

The process that has guided my journey is there for anyone and everyone who chooses to start and/or continue their journey. Because I needed a fundamental shift in all areas of my life, I took an approach that encompassed my body, mind, and spirit.

- *A commitment to recondition my body.* I committed to a personal exercise program to train my muscles and renew the life in my body.

- *A commitment to train my mind.* I committed to sessions with David initially focused on stress and weight loss. I decided to continue with David as my mind coach and my guide to learn to use my subconscious and conscious minds so that I could choose my thoughts, emotions, and behaviors. I learned to let go of anger and fear. I said to myself, "Oh really?" And I answered silently to myself, "Yes, dear skeptic, I know you."

- *A commitment to the program.* From my perspective, my experience of David's program, The Best Me NOW!, has been all about awareness, discovery, going within to know myself, and learning to love myself. This is exactly why I have chosen to share my journal entries. Now I want to see if my journal may help you feel the path I was walking. David did not tell me what to do or what to feel. He is a guide – simply by asking questions. I take it from there, integrating exactly the issues I want to address. I learn what I experience and I experience what I learn.

- *A commitment to God.* I committed to a daily focus on spiritual renewal to get in touch with God the Father, the Son, and the Holy Spirit, and the Great Mother of the *Tao Te Ching.*

In retrospect, it was a holistic process. The new life in my body reinvigorated my mind. The new training of my mind and emotional control opened the path to my spiritual journey of forgiveness and unconditional love, seeing God in everyone and everything. I desired to truly, deeply, spiritually, and eternally come home and to unconditionally love myself.

My approach, my steps, and my tactics were—and still are—a good fit for me. For me, it was a way to become more aware, to discover the *me* inside myself by engaging my conscious and subconscious mind. I learned through experiencing, through feeling the lessons. David's process of The Best Me NOW! has worked for me, and it has worked for thousands of people.

In the very first year, the early stages of my new journey, I made more than thirty changes to my daily practices and the way I lived my life, ranging from the very simple to the profound. I document the list of changes and choices in the appendix simply because it is hard to believe that any person can effect so much change in a short period of time and without a plan.

I invite you to walk with me. Reflect. How does this relate to your journey? Take your own key and open the doors of your conscious and subconscious minds. The changes you want in your life can truly shift instantaneously once your perception changes.

Skeptical? I certainly was. As a securities analyst, I have an advanced degree in skepticism. Plus I was born and raised in New York City. *Tell me about it!*

I invite you to walk with us and see the unfolding of the process through my eyes and experiences. I hope to reveal how my defenses dropped away and how I was transformed and fully returned to life in a very deep and profound way.

***

Let us start by taking the sixteen steps up to my third-floor office, which is also transformed. As we reach the top step, a huge round window opens to a spectacular view of Lake Erie. We are probably sixty feet above Lake Erie with a 180 degree landscape of water and sky, islands, and boats. Herons, seagulls, and even the occasional eagle soar by.

In my old cramped office, my computer and workstation faced a wall and were surrounded by filing cabinets and walls decked out with plaques and awards. The computer workstation is now angled to look out over the lake. We created a new sitting area for reading and meetings with clients by utilizing the French doors, which open onto a third-floor deck with new planters and bird feeders. The entire loft was opened up to allow wonderful energy to flow from the round window facing the gardens to the front round window looking out on the lake with glorious sunsets. Over time I have added a couple of altars for meditation on spirituality and relationships. We gradually replaced most of the financial books with new readings we will discuss later. I took the certificates down, replaced them with a bulletin board of pictures of family and friends and beautiful places I had traveled to. Welcome to my writer's loft. Welcome to my new life.

What did I learn? How did I learn? How did I experience and feel the breakthroughs?

It is important to start with the six most important lessons learned. Everyone likes lists, right?

I believe the value of sharing my journey and journal entries is the sharing of the *how*. How did I learn? How did I come to experience the important universal truths of letting go, forgiveness, and unconditional love?

What did I learn? As I discussed in the introduction, my top six experiential lessons are as follows:

1. "The Power to Choose": I learned how to take back control of my thoughts and how to choose to live a healthier and happier life.

2. "Let Go and Take Control": I learned how to let go of old hurts and anger and the suffering of losing a loved one.

3. "Forgive and Be Free": I learned how to forgive myself and others.

4. "Release and Rejoice": I learned how to release deep-seated fears.

43

5. "Look Within and Love Me": I learned how to find peace in the present moment and what it feels like to unconditionally love yourself and others. I discovered my purpose.

6. "I Am Not Special": I learned how to tap into my Higher Spirit and how to connect with everyone by seeing we are all the same. God is in everyone, everything, and everywhere. I learned that I am unique rather than special.

I will share some of my journal entries and words and feelings that came together as I experienced the lessons. What ideas does this give you about your journey?

There are both instantaneous changes and evolutionary changes, and there are also regressions and the need to learn some lessons over again.

I chose one day in May. I connected with David Prudhomme and his process, The Best Me NOW!, to change my life, to change from where I was to where I really wanted to be.

Mind you, David never mentioned his proprietary program, and for good reason. If David had laid out the program and the process, it would have been another checklist. I would have looked through the entire list and thought, *Yeah, yeah, yeah. I got it.* As my guide, David simply allowed me to experience whatever I experienced, and then and only then did I *get it!*

Got it? It is about the experience, and that is the most important reason why I have chosen to share my journey and my journal entries. It is a gift from my heart.

Let us fast-forward and take a glimpse of just how far and deep the journey progressed in just one year.

***

On the one-year anniversary of the start of my journey, David sent me a text to give me more insight into what happened to me on 9/11 and how that had led to my journey of self-discovery. David wrote,

> On September 11th 2001, Osama bin Laden introduced "fear" into the daily lives of every single American ... For the first time in history every American knew they were vulnerable ... If the World Trade Centers could be destroyed ... then anywhere is unsafe ... Alison ... the shock of 9/11 was a feeling of "fear" and unsafe ... That was a pattern interruption for you.
>
> That's how we all experience fear and negative pattern interruptions ... We state to ourselves ... what I know to be true is no longer true ... how I live my life, what I believe is out the window ... I need to reassess ... I need to figure out what's really going on ... I need to figure out myself ... my world ... my part ... my joy ... my happiness ... my contribution ... my purpose ... my meaning ... my peace ... MY absence of fear.

David knew this to be true for me and for everyone.

It had taken me almost nine years to get from knowing when to stop (my pattern interruption) to the official May 3 start of my journey.

Then in one incredible year, the best year of my life ever, I moved on to all the really profound issues—meaning, purpose, the absence of fear, the feeling of joy and compassion, and love.

I hope my journey of body, mind, and spiritual renewal will reveal a process that you can use to change your life and achieve your highest aspirations. Be happy *now*, not tomorrow or next year or when you turn fifty-something or when you fall in love or when you do this or that.

Happiness is already there right *now* inside of you. This I *Know*.

It is very important to fully understand why *Know* is capitalized in this last sentence. This is intentional and a very important lesson I learned from David early on in our sessions and in later philosophical discussions.

What is the difference between *Believing* and *Knowing*? Personally, I have always thought that believing in a Higher Power and God was a beautiful leap of faith. Over time I meandered from a religious, tutored faith to questioning to a lack of faith to a nascent return to a belief in angels and life hereafter to where I am in my journey today—a deeply spiritual and religious person.

In one of our early discussions, David said he *Knows*. I challenge him. How could he possibly *Know*? Where was the proof, the research, the scientific facts?

David started to help me understand there is a very important difference between *Believing* and *Knowing*. The key difference is that in *Knowing*, there is not one iota of doubt. There is no leap of faith.

At the outset I did not get it. Be patient. As my story unfolds, I gradually learn and experience what it means to truly *Know*. As I will reveal in the chapter "Look Within and Love Me," I recognize my purpose. I *Know* it is my soul purpose. I don't just Believe it is my purpose. I *Know* in the core of my Being, my soul, that it is my purpose.

Perhaps knowing and purpose are a little too abstract or *out there*. There is another great example of what it really means to *Know* in the chapter "Lessons from Golf." In Dr. Rotella's story about the mind of Jack Nicklaus, Jack *Knew* in his mind what was true.

Happiness is already there right *now* inside of you. This I *Know*!

CHAPTER 5

The Power to Choose

The power of decision is my own.

—*A Course in Miracles*, Lesson 152

Working on Wall Street, rising to be a managing director and one of a handful of women at the top level of a global investment banking organization, I knew how to handle stress. I knew how to handle conflict. I knew how to handle the vagaries of the markets and professional change. Right? Wrong!

Learning I have the power to choose was the first and remains one of the most powerful lessons of my journey. At the start, I was focused on stress and weight loss. I was not expecting to be on a journey. I just wanted to look and feel better. Don't we all? Haven't we all read hundreds of books and seen programs on this issue? I had heard from a couple of friends that David's approach was uniquely different and that it worked. I could see the results in my friends after just two sessions with David.

How did I learn that I have the power to choose? Instantly. Slowly. Repeatedly. I know this sounds paradoxical. Let me share my journey of realizing that I do indeed have the power to choose my thoughts, emotions, and behaviors.

After my very first session with David, changes I wanted to see happened instantaneously. As I committed myself to a journey leading to my real Self in order to control my actions and reactions, I realized there are layers upon layers upon layers to my mind. There was a gradual process of learning and exploring a range of emotions and past habits of behavior as David guided me deeper and deeper into the early origins of my emotions.

Sometimes—honestly, many times—I have to learn the lesson over and over because the patterns of behavior and emotion are deeply ingrained. At least now I am aware and have the ability to make midcourse corrections. We are all unique and complex individuals. We are not two-dimensional caricatures of our public persona. We all have many layers. From my perspective, some lessons are easier to learn than others. Some lessons go very deep to the core of who I thought I was, and the unlearning and the relearning process takes longer and requires more iterations.

Sometimes David and I will joke—after it has taken me time to regroup—that I need to go back and reread the chapters "The Power to Choose" and "Let Go and Take Control." This is why I say learning that I have the power to choose came instantly, slowly, and repeatedly.

Since it all starts with the mind, it is important to demystify and address a few typical questions. What is David's approach from the client's perspective? What is the role of the hypnosis? Is it tapping into the conscious and the subconscious minds? Am I really in control?

In brief, David Prudhomme integrated the latest scientific research on the mind-body connection with my goals and helped me reprogram my subconscious along the lines we had discussed and agreed upon in the pre-talk. And yes, I was totally in control of my mind. What else would you expect from a self-diagnosed control freak?

***

As alluded to in the last chapter, after the initial interrogatory, the "getting to know you" part of the meeting, David and I started to talk about stress and weight loss and the latest scientific and medical research on the mind-body connection.

In our pre-talk, David discussed the interrelationship of stress to overall health and wellness. He talked about how stress affects the body on every level—physically, mentally, and emotionally—and taught me how to take manual control of my autonomic nervous system by using my breathing. David instructed me to do my breathing in the morning when I got up, at night when I went to bed, and at least seven times a day. More on this later. The breathing I understand. Well, I never heard of the autonomic nervous system on Wall Street.

On food, diet, and nutrition, the discussions were very specific. David shared the latest research on how food affects the body. He was very clear about eliminating sugar, most processed foods, eating only foods that were once alive, only eating when you are hungry, and stopping when you are satisfied.

After the interrogatory, I was *satisfied* that David had done his research on the science of weight loss and stress and the mind-body connection. It was just like I was probing a CEO on his or her strategy and rationale for a company's transformation. In the past, some CEOs and CFOs had called my boss to register a complaint. I had asked too many questions, and they were offended. David had already spent at least two hours with me. I was persistent, inquisitive, relentless, and skeptical. David was patient, willing to share his knowledge and caring, infinitely caring about me and what I had shared and what I hoped to change.

What did I have to lose? Deep down, I knew that I was desperate. I was not happy with who I had become. I knew I must reconnect with who I really am. And who am I really? I could not answer that question at that point.

This was my first experience with sessions that involved both the conscious and the subconscious minds. The subconscious mind? Is that hypnosis? I had very few preconceived notions, although many people do have visions of stage hypnosis and fears of clucking like a chicken. The main issue for me was trusting someone with my mind. In the process I learned I was actually trusting myself with my own mind, and David was teaching me how to take back control of my mind. Imagine that!

The session started with David guiding me through conscious breathing and relaxation techniques into a deep state of trance much like a daydream. I was, indeed, as David said, relaxed and aware the entire time. I heard David talking to me. He was talking about *all* of the points of our discussion, exactly what I said I wanted to change. It was a smooth integration of my personal goals and his advice for me to make the desired changes in my lifestyle and habits.

As I emerged from the session, I felt more relaxed than I could ever remember. I felt like a baby waking up from a nap.

As every session came to a close, David asked me to finish two sentences with the first thought that comes to my mind. David said, "Repeat after me and finish this sentence 'I have changed because now I *Know* ...'"

I have changed because now I *Know* ... I can change!

Next David said, "Repeat after me and finish this sentence. 'I have changed because now I *Feel*...'"

I have changed because now I *Feel* ... happier!

By design, my session—indeed, as David tells me, all sessions—concluded this way for a couple of very good reasons. First, I have no time to think, so I naturally tap into my subconscious mind with clarity of thought about the most important points I now *Know* and I now *Feel*. Second, this practice solidifies in my mind the subconscious themes and feelings I will take with me as I leave the session, and these are now always with me.

In this first session, I learned that I was in control. My initial fear that I was giving up control and giving someone else access to and power over my mind was totally wrong. There it was again. I was wrong. The super smart, analytical Wall Street securities strategist ... was wrong.

Learning was a humbling experience and an opportunity to grow. Even more amazing, I emerged from the session knowing that I could control my mind and my body. Rather than reacting to people and situations based on old habits and patterns, I had learned that I could choose my emotions, thoughts, and behaviors.

As I left the office and drove home, I immediately started to do my breathing. I was calmer and more relaxed than I had felt in years and years. I looked in the mirror when I got home. My face looked different!

Can you see your stress when you look in the mirror? Imagine seeing yourself totally relaxed and not stressed.

I could *see* it. That very night I started sleeping better and drinking less wine. That very next day, I started eating healthier. That week the pounds started melting away. The changes were happening seemingly automatically.

My skeptical, analytical mind was amazed that personal change could be instantaneous. I was now more in control than I had ever been in my whole life.

***

In my first two sessions with David, the connection for me between stress and weight loss was very clear. They are inextricably intertwined. I must be able to control my stress better in order to be successful in the long term with weight management. David reassured me that was quite normal.

Focus on Breathing

David talked at length in the first session about the importance of breathing. His guidance to me was to breathe deeply from the stomach at least seven times a day for at least three minutes.

I was doing a lot of breathing—in the morning, in the evening, every time I started the car, every time I got impatient, every time I got angry, every time I was frustrated. Now that is a lot of breathing. Perhaps it helps explain where I was stress-wise at that point in my life.

David explained that breathing with my diaphragm creates a relaxation response in both my body and my mind. The relaxation response is the opposite of the "flight or fight" response, which generates an increase in cortisol and causes the body to retain fat. This is part of the science behind the enormous benefits of diaphragmatic breathing. Indeed, my personal experience bears out these scientific findings. The more I learn how to relax my body and my mind when there is little stress, the better I am at being able to be calm and relax my body and mind when moments of stress, frustration, anger, or fear arise.

Breathing was a simple step, and it was huge. It was huge because it started the learning process and the experience of taking back control of my body, my mind, and my emotions.

Focus on Gratitude

David suggested that I start my day with breathing and also gratitude, specifically choosing at least three things I am grateful for that day. I instantly connected with the relationship of gratitude and prayer. I have often started my day with prayer to find the comfort of the Lord, even if it is only reciting my Hail Mary and the Lord's Prayer. This suggestion made my prayers more heartfelt and more specific, and it helped me start my day in gratitude rather than in stress, thinking about my long to-do list for that day.

Thus, I began to start my days when I first open my eyes with three expressions of gratitude. The three things I choose evolve and vary—family, friends, nature and events.

One day almost five months into this new daily gratitude practice, I chose to be grateful for *me*. I was thankful to be me, thankful for my life. Imagine that! This was the first glimmer of understanding that gratitude is an attitude, a way of living that includes everyone and everything, most especially *me*.

Focus on Eating Healthy

Like so many people, I have tried a range of diets. Many diets work for a time, and then the pounds creep back on. I know that I use eating as a reflex to try to relieve stress. Of course, it just adds to the stress because now I feel I am a *bad girl*, overindulging in eating and drinking wine.

These are a few of the things I really like in David's approach.

- It is specific. I identified specific foods and types of foods that I knew were not healthy and that I wanted to let go of. In my case, I decided it was important to cut back on dairy products and fat in my daily eating habits. I used half-and-half in my coffee, sour cream with my salsa and chips, and rich sauces with the meats I prepare. I was very good about not eating junk food with two important exceptions—Big Macs and Cheetos. I was not very good about limiting my wine consumption. I decided to limit my wine consumption to a maximum of two glasses a day. Some might say this is still too much. For me, it is where I started. David incorporated this into my session, and there is not even a whiff of judgment.

- There are no rules in the sense of counting carbs, calories, or points or weighing ounces of meat.

- The guidelines are simple and straightforward. Eat only when I am hungry. Stop eating when I am satisfied.

- The guidelines are also backed by scientific research. Eat only things that were once alive. Eliminate or substantially reduce refined and processed foods. Eliminate or substantially reduce intake of sugar. I do not use sugar in my coffee. I do not have a sweet tooth, and I learned to read labels and see how much sugar is in so many supposedly healthy foods as well as in processed foods. David has focused on the health risks of sugar for many years, long before Dr. Oz labeled it "the #1 food you want out of your house!"

It works! It really is amazing. I was not fighting myself anymore. My conscious and subconscious minds were aligned. It all came naturally. In the six months following my first session with David, I lost thirty pounds without dieting. The new me was starting to emerge, and I felt great! How could this be happening? Read on.

***

Ever the analyst, I wanted to know why and how David's process worked with such amazing consistency and success with clients. One key element is the dismissal of willpower and the focus on reprogramming my subconscious. As David explained, willpower resides in the conscious mind, which is only 10 percent of your mind. I stopped judging myself and condemning myself for all the past slips and failings of willpower. Releasing guilt was powerful.

Rather the focus was on my subconscious. David explained to me that the subconscious is actually 90 percent of the mind. With David's guidance and my input, we reprogrammed my subconscious mind through hypnosis to incorporate my new healthy eating habits. It is very important to understand this approach is not like a diet. I was choosing to let go of unhealthy eating habits. Now my conscious and subconscious minds were on the same track.

Another key to my success was my level of commitment. A couple of months before I saw David, I started to work out at a local fitness center. First, I committed to a three-to-five-day cardio program and then moved on to work with a personal trainer for strength and conditioning. I was committed to recovering some level of fitness. Growing up, I was the *jock*. I played on the JV and varsity teams in field hockey, volleyball, basketball, and gymnastics. I was the tennis champ. I was voted "most athletic" in my senior year of high school. I love sports, and I know what it feels like to be fit. However, in those two months of training while I started to feel my muscle tone improve, I did not lose any weight.

By the time I was ready to start with David, I was deeply committed to changing my life, taking back control of my life and looking and feeling better. The most important point is that was simple for me to do and to understand.

***

My second session was designed to reinforce the new healthy eating habits and enhance my ability to reduce my stress. David also explained this session would incorporate guided visualization and future pacing. It is a good thing David didn't tell me ahead of time about the techniques because I would have been Googling the terms and would have totally lost focus on the objective of the process, namely changing my thoughts, behaviors, and emotions.

David explained that he was going to give me another tool that I could use when I did my breathing to reduce my stress as well as reenergize and reinforce the changes I had made. In the session he would guide me to create in my mind a beautiful, peaceful, relaxing, special place that I could visit anytime. While there, he would reinforce all of my changes, and I would see myself happier and healthier in the future. David would use guided visualization and future pacing to empower my subconscious mind to consistently and constantly draw me to who and where I want to be.

In this session, I created a beautiful meadow of flowers. The colors were dazzling. I was wandering in the meadow, basking in the sun with a gentle breeze blowing on my face. There were no bees or insects here, not in my beautiful place. I was smiling and skipping. I was happy. As I am writing this paragraph, I can close my eyes and transport myself to this lovely meadow of wildflowers. I now know I can go to this place anytime and anywhere to relax and to center myself regardless of what is going on around me. Right now it is of no consequence that it is actually a brutally bitter cold winter day and the wind is howling around my third-floor writer's loft. I feel warm and content.

What does your beautiful, peaceful, relaxing special place look like? Imagine yourself there now. How do you feel? What are you thinking, and most importantly, what are you thinking about yourself?

I was still in trance. David guided me to see myself after all my changes. I looked three months in the future and then six months in the future and then one year in the future. What I saw was an amazing transformation. At each and every point, I was thinner and healthier and happier. At the one-year point, I was on a cloud, dancing, hands outstretched to a beautiful clear blue sky, feeling joy and peace. In my picture, I was wearing a white sundress. I was thinner and healthier, and my muscles were supple. My hair was dark brown, long, and flowing in the wind. I was radiating light. I was truly, deeply happy.

In that session I future-paced my new reality. My subconscious mind, through my own guidance, shaped my personal transformation. I am now living one of my dreams, writing this book and sharing my story of personal transformation. I am in the best shape of my life—physically, mentally, and emotionally.

As I emerged from my trance fully awake and aware, David asked me to complete the two key sentences with the first thought that comes to mind.

I have changed because now I *Know* … who I am!

I have changed because now I *Feel* … joy!

How I completed these two key sentences continues to leave me in awe. They are always very revealing. I started to discover at a very deep level who I knew myself to be. I understood at a very deep emotional level what joy actually felt like in my body.

I just recently realized that my hair is now long and dark brown, my original hair color. It is truly amazing how the subconscious mind works. I feel more like my true self, the me who was always there.

If you were to imagine yourself happier and healthier, making all the changes you wanted to make in your life, how would you see yourself ... three months from now? Six months from now? One year from now?

What changes have you or will you make? How are you taking better care of yourself a year from now?

Ali's List of Changes and Choices

As I discuss each step on the journey, I give examples of some of the changes I start to incorporate in my life. (See the Appendix, "Ali's List of Changes and Choices," for the compilation of the most important and even a few trivial examples of the scope of my transformation.)

From these two sessions on stress and weight loss, the list begins.

1. I started eating a healthier diet with less dairy, less pasta, less bread. I started eating foods that had been alive and avoiding processed foods. For example, I no longer add half-and-half to my coffee. It may sound like a small change; however, given the amount of half-and-half I was using at the start of every day, it is a very important change for me.

2. I started beginning every day when I first open my eyes with three expressions of gratitude. The three things I choose evolve and vary—family, friends, nature, and events.

3. I started losing weight (thirty pounds).

4. I started drinking less wine. I enjoyed wine to connect with people, not to hide from people or situations.

5. I started getting my hair cut on a regular basis rather than using my former last-minute and irregular scheduling.

6. I started stopping a decades-long habit of biting my nails. A French manicure was a celebration, and it was the start of caring for my hands.

7. I started taking better care of my body and getting massages as a regular practice, not a perk.

8. I continued with a cardio and weight regimen. It is now part of my routine and self-care.

This was a great start! Guess what? At that point, I still did not realize what was happening that summer. A journey? I never really thought about it at the time.

I was in the moment, and I loved every minute of the learning and the revelations and the freedom. David simply said after receiving one of my texts, "Glad to hear you are enjoying your path. Keep walking and doing your breathing. Namaste."

Ali's Testimonial

A fitting close to this chapter is a testimonial I wrote to David that summer. My testimonial acknowledges the new path I was on and foreshadows the changes that have just started to emerge and the changes that are to follow.

Dear David,

In my sessions with you, I have experienced several *shazam* moments of revelation, including the following:

- My greatest resource is me. I can learn a lot from my inner self.

- A new piece in the mosaic of my life and my commitment to lifelong learning is the discovery of looking inward, utilizing hypnosis, and training my mind.

- When I let go, when I step outside myself, I increase my control over situations and my emotions.

- I am never alone. I may be by myself, but I am never alone. I am always with me, and my Higher Power, God, is always with me.

I am now achieving my personal goals of weight loss and stress management and rediscovering the joy and love in me.

With no overstatement, this is the best summer of my life.

Sincerely, thankfully, joyfully,
Ali

This is my testimonial to give thanks for all the changes I have made with the guidance and support of David Prudhomme. This testimonial also hints at the many changes to come as I go deeper and deeper within and get to know my inner Self, who I truly am and always was.

It is all about learning and practicing and experiencing the power to choose.

CHAPTER 6

Let Go and Take Control

For every minute you are angry
you lose sixty seconds of happiness.

—Ralph Waldo Emerson

Let go and take control. It appears paradoxical.

In my professional career, the ability to plan, the insight to anticipate problems and opportunities, and my natural instinct to get ahead of the curve were skills that were praised and highlighted. In my personal life, the ability to host dinner parties with flair and ease where everything is carefully planned and prepared ahead of time has been widely complimented.

But on the other side of the coin, I have sometimes been labeled a "control freak." I liked to think of it all as a careful and masterful orchestration of next steps or events. After all, who likes surprises? Certainly not me … in most situations. I had a tight grip on the throttle on my life. Where is the joy and happiness in this approach? What are the underlying driving forces and emotions? Deeply buried anger and resentment perhaps?

In the last chapter, I started to learn how to take control of my thoughts and behavior, to reduce stress and lose weight. Terrific!

I have the power to choose, right?

I was learning that I was always in control. Yes, I was learning, and I still have a lot to learn.

Now I was going to learn how to let go. How does that make any sense?

Well, to choose a new emotion usually means that I must let go of the initial thought and emotion. As Emerson wrote so many years ago, "For every moment you are angry you lose sixty seconds of happiness."

***

David, my guide and my mind coach who instructed me during the initial sessions with both the conscious and subconscious levels of my mind, was instrumental to my taking back control of my life. My journey continued and went even deeper when David asked, "What would you think about doing a couple of additional sessions on some of your negative emotions and limiting beliefs about yourself that you have accumulated over your lifetime? What is the most uncomfortable emotion you experience?"

Hmm … I needed some time to reflect on that gentle suggestion.

David had been coaching me that there is only one choice for me to make in any situation. Do I choose love or fear? He continued to elaborate and give examples of how emotions are choices. Did I already know from scripture and pastoral teachings that the opposite of love is not hate? Yes, I had heard that the opposite of love is not hate but fear. Intellectually, I understood that.

However, as I wrote in my journal, I thought, *If I were to move forward and start to probe emotional issues, where would I start? Anger? Fear?*

I privately acknowledged that I was a deeply angry and fearful person. I needed to be in control of everything and everyone. Being in control is my offense and my defense. When I was in control, I was managing others, my priorities, and my schedule with a focus on results. Control was also my defense. It was how I kept distance between myself and others and how I tried to keep my demons and my fears at bay.

I figured that anger, resentment, and fear were feeding my stress.

For me, this was an important decision. Should I move forward and continue to work with David? I did some reading as I pondered my answer to David's suggestion. I picked up a book from David's library of resources at Mederi Wellness titled *The Secret Language of Feelings* by Calvin Banyan. I understood that I was not knowledgeable about feelings. I would rather do almost anything than talk about my feelings. In my early family history, talk, and especially talk about feelings, never resulted in anything constructive, only in going in circles, crying jags, and hurt feelings.

I had a flashback to an experience very early in my career. I was at Continental Bank during the eve of the largest bank failure and FDIC bailout at the time. It was almost 11:00 p.m. The deal needed to close by midnight. There were all kinds of last-minute issues and crises. In the director's room, there was our outside counsel, a person who went on to become one of the most famous and successful lawyers in bank bailouts, mergers, and acquisitions in our time. He had a line of people waiting to talk with him. I am guessing the line stretched to at least forty people, and I was at the back of the line. The attorney motioned me forward. He knew my question was likely to be critical to the composition of the loan portfolio to be transferred at midnight. We spoke briefly and resolved the point.

Later during that very long night around 2:00 a.m., after the deal had closed, I had a private moment to ask him, "How do you do it?" I asked this because emotions had been running high. People were yelling. Some were crying. Everyone in line thought they were the most important person, and they were angry. The attorney's answer has stayed with me always. "The more chaotic events and the more emotional people become, the calmer I become." Wow! It was amazing to see him put this philosophy into action. With a calm mind, he could think clearly, and he kept all the other peoples' emotions at bay. This attorney was in control of his actions; he did not react to other people's emotions or to the events swirling around him.

I tried to learn from this experience. See the chapter titled "Lessons on Self-Talk." I tried to put this lesson into practice. In fact, as events unfolded, some people at the bank remarked at how calm I sometimes appeared amidst the turmoil of one market crisis after another, one more management reorganization, one more restructuring, one more acquisition, etc. There were endless opportunities to practice being calm in the midst of crisis.

To make this long story short, I had a major realization. I was only calm on the surface. Below the surface my emotions were raging. It was an exercise in outward self-control. I was not really in control.

And so after reading and reflecting, I decided to continue a few more sessions with David in order to focus on my emotions—emotional intelligence and emotional control.

Certainly, I had started to see great results after my initial sessions on weight loss and stress. David's gentle suggestion to look deeper into the emotional issues resonated, and I was starting to develop a deeper level of trust in David's guidance and experience. At some level, I had let down just enough barriers to acknowledge that going more deeply within on the issue of anger would be an important next step and helpful to me in managing stress. I knew I had kept emotions bottled up for years. I was just starting to understand the toll that stress and anger was taking on me, on my health, on my outlook on life, and on my happiness ... or lack thereof.

I put my pride and my ego aside, at least in part, and suggested to David that we start to explore my repressed emotion of anger.

This was both my final frontier and the early beginnings of my journey inward and my awakening. The floodgates had opened even wider. I was going deeper and deeper within.

I Am an Angry and Controlling Person

Ouch! It even hurts to write that heading. It was the truth at the time.

Why was I angry? Was I right in being angry?

In the talk before my session, David asked me to select the most uncomfortable emotion I experienced. I chose repressed anger. David asked, "When you experience anger, where do you feel it in your body?"

And I answered, "I feel it in my stomach. My stomach is in a knot with a fist inside. My face is flushed. My eyes are teary."

David explained that all emotions reside in the subconscious mind, and in fact, the subconscious mind is organized by emotion. Throughout our lifetimes we develop patterns—patterns of emotions, patterns of thought, and patterns of behavior. We think this is who we are because that is what we have experienced; however, they are just patterns, and these patterns can be easily changed.

In this session I was going to trace back my experience of feeling angry to its origin so that I could cut the thread that tied me to my past emotional patterns of behavior. I liked these rather extensive discussions because it gave me a better understanding of the process as well as an opportunity to ask questions. I almost always had questions. Imagine that!

In session David guided me deep into my subconscious, to feel the emotions, to experience the visceral sense of my anger—the knot in my stomach, the fist, the flush on my face. As the feelings arose within my body, he instructed me to follow the feelings back to the first time I ever had that feeling in my body. The feelings continued to grow stronger, and he guided me further back into my childhood to the first time I was extremely angry. "Be there. First impression. Is it daytime or nighttime? Are you inside or outside? Are you alone or with someone? How old are you?" David was guiding me to bring up both the emotion of anger and a very specific first memory of feeling angry. I was there!

It is insightful that leading up to this session, I initially thought it would be a tough choice. How would I decide on the focal point of my feelings of anger? There were so many choices—family, friends, and business associates, screaming syndicate managers and traders.

However, in hypnosis, my subconscious mind went directly to the first time I felt really angry. It was evening. I was in the upstairs bedroom, ready for bed. My mother and older sister were in the room. I was five years old. What follows is a combination of David's notes and my recollections of this session.

> Mom is yelling, screaming at me.
> Mom is hitting my legs really hard, with two large, thin
> books as I lay crouched in my bed.
>
> Why is Mom so angry? I may have told her she is a bad
> mother.
> I am crying so hard. I do not remember.
> Most likely, I had lied to her.
> I am hurting.
> I am a bad girl.
> Mom doesn't love me.
> Through my wails of "You are hurting me," Mom stops.
> I remember that I pretended that she caused me real pain.
> I get out of bed and walk with a limp.
> I am manipulating her and trying to make her feel
> guilty and ashamed.

The session continued, and the process was carefully conducted. This was where David's art and his intuitive skills shined because it was so dynamic and unique to my experience. In hindsight I now understand that he was guiding me to reframe my memory of this experience with all that I knew at this point in my life.

71

The next and critically important step in the process was to have five-year-old Lil' Ali go back to earlier in the evening before the incident ever happened, a time when everything was fine. At this point David said, "Alison, follow my instructions immediately and instantly. Grown-up Alison, you are now there with Lil' Ali, standing next to her bed." I was there! I saw the five-year-old me, Lil' Ali. She looked up at me and smiled sweetly. I smiled back. I felt a deep love for her.

David said, "Wouldn't it have been nice to know back then what you know now? Wouldn't that have made things easier?"

Of course, the answer is yes.

I then took on the responsibility to tell five-year-old Lil' Ali exactly what was going to happen to her that night. I told her what she needed to know to get through that experience without feeling hurt or angry or that she was a bad girl or that her mother did not love her. David was guiding me, and he asked, "If that was your little girl, what would you tell her?"

I knew I was crying. The tears were flowing. The emotions were starting to release. I loved that little girl. Grown-up Alison sat on the side of the bed and smiled down on Lil' Ali. I said the following:

> I will always be there for you.
> I understand you.
> I love you.
> I know the games you can play. You are very smart.
> I know your limping is mostly an act. That is okay.

I know you do not really want to hurt anyone, even if
you feel hurt.
I know Mom truly and deeply loves you, and she will
do anything she can to make you happy.
All right, maybe you misbehaved. Maybe Mom lost
patience with you.
I know Mom loves you, and I know you love Mom.

These notes only capture the essence of the process. The actual length
of this session lasted almost forty-five minutes. In the interest of
privilege and privacy, I am leaving a lot out. Mom almost never hit me.
Mom was an amazing and caring mother, yet this session brought to
the surface so many emotions. There was anger, embarrassment, guilt,
resentment, and judgment. Most importantly, there was also a deep
and abiding love.

I am sharing both my experience as well as David's design of this
process, which guided me to make myself *whole*, to release that part of
me that was feeling unworthy or "not good enough." I was talking to
Lil' Ali, and by healing Lil' Ali, I was healing myself. I was letting go of
negative and limiting beliefs. I was letting go of the deep-seated anger
I had carried with me for so many years.

Let us pause for a moment and reflect. Who knows better how to heal
yourself than you? This process is not someone telling you what to do
or how to do it. There is not a checklist that you can simply check off
and move on. This process is you talking, and it teaches you what you
already really *know* in your own subconscious.

And so in this session, by going back to a moment in time early in my
life and cutting the cord to that deep-seated emotion of anger, I let go.

73

I healed myself. Even more importantly, I learned how to heal myself. Anytime I feel anger welling up inside of me, I know exactly what I feel and where I feel it in my body. With breathing and stepping aside, I know I can and will let go of the anger because I choose to no longer hurt myself. Do I need to practice this lesson? Absolutely! Do I get better with practice? Yes.

At the end of this session (and every session), David asked me to complete the following sentences: I have changed because:

> Now I *Know* … I deserve to treat myself right.
> Now I *Feel* … I love myself.

When I released old emotions of anger, I knew I deserved to treat myself right. I felt I did love myself. These statements explicitly show the realization from deep within that my anger was only hurting me.

There it was. Let go of my anger and stop hurting myself. Choose to be good to myself and love myself. When I let go of my anger, I am free to choose the emotions of self-respect and love.

After that second statement, as I was emerging from hypnosis, I added, *"From this day forward, I will use all of my talents, all of my abilities, and all of my resources to help all people … not just certain people but all people."*

Wow! Where did that come from? This was a message from very deep in my heart and in my soul. In fact, it is the statement of my soul purpose, and it took me another six months to understand this realization. In the chapter titled "Look Within and Love Me," we will come back and explore this major self-realization in some detail.

At that time, I was processing so much from this session, and I simply shrugged my shoulders and thought to myself, *Well, that's nice.*

The reality is that emotions are choices is a lesson I will have to learn again and again and again. Emotions take on many forms. There are so many subtleties and so many different situations. The lesson is always the same. The lesson is very simple. Do I choose love? Or do I choose fear?

***

I want to share a very personal story and revelation about how I am learning in so many ways and in so many different situations to choose love over fear ... always.

Zacharia, our twelve-year-old chocolate Lab with an incredibly loving and strong heart, was failing. It was getting close to his time. In his honor and now in his memory, I share this journal entry about letting go of other emotions related to anger and fear, such as sadness, suffering, longing, loneliness, and loss. He taught me a lesson of love and helped me to experience love in a profound way.

> *Ali*: Very early one morning, around 3:30 a.m., I am wandering around the house. Suffering, longing, loneliness, and loss are filling my mind.
> I go back to bed, and Zacharia puts his head on my leg, rolls on his back, and puts his feet in the air, an invitation to rub his belly. I can feel his heart beating. All I can think about is unconditional love. I know Zacharia loves me unconditionally. I love him unconditionally.

I continue to gently rub his belly and whisper softly, "I love you, Zacharia." This connection goes on for some time. Now I get it. Where love is, there is nothing else. Loss, loneliness, longing cannot exist where love reigns supreme.

I choose love, not fear.

Later, that very morning, I opened to *A Course in Miracles*, and found Lesson 152.

The power of decision is my own. No one can suffer loss unless it be his own decision. No one suffers pain except his choice elects this state for him. No one can grieve nor fear nor think him sick unless there are outcomes that he wants.

Thank you, Zacharia. You helped me experience this important lesson on a very deep level. The only choice is truly between love or fear.

To choose love, I must let go of anger, resentment, loneliness, loss— you name it! I can and will choose love only when I have let go of all negative and limiting emotions and beliefs.

When I let go, I take control, and then I have the power and the freedom to truly choose from a loving heart.

Ali's List of Changes and Choices

1. Reading and meditating every morning is now the way I choose to start my day. I used to start my day with the Weather Channel, CNBC, and the *Wall Street Journal*. What will the weather be for my commute? What is the breaking news in the market? Oh,

shit! What do I have to deal with now? This daily routine was the practice in my days on Wall Street. I had not varied from that routine in the nine years since I had left the Street. Now for at least an hour with no TV, I sit with my cup of coffee and read and meditate. Silence. Peace. Gratitude.

2. I have started integrating more music into my life and much less TV. Music lifts my spirit and my soul. I have started buying and playing Steven Halpern CDs, such as *Chakra Suite* and *Music for Sound Healing*. I have started going to local concerts, and if I am going by myself, that is okay. I find this music is calming and healing and transporting. One of my most recent discoveries is a lovely CD with Celtic harp by Lisa Lynn Franco and a bamboo flute by George Tortorelli titled *Love and Peace*. It is heavenly.

3. I have been controlling my mind, training my mind to dismiss echoes of my past, focusing and centering myself in order to stay in the present.

4. I have started choosing love, not fear.

CHAPTER 7

Forgive and Be Free

Judge not, and you shall not be judged.
Condemn not, and you shall not be condemned.
Forgive, and you will be forgiven;
give and it will be given to you.

—Jesus of Nazareth, Luke 6:37–38

As I write this chapter and review my journal notes, I see that I do not even know how to spell "forgiveness." All my journal entries write about "foregiveness." It's not just an occasional typo; it is in my handwritten journal notations over and over.

If I do not know how to even spell *forgiveness* correctly, what does that say about my understanding and practice of forgiveness? Perhaps it means nothing. Perhaps it says something very important.

I believe there is a very deep message for me. I have been a student of the art of communicating for my entire professional career. When I can't find exactly the right word or I cannot remember a definition of a word or I consistently misspell a word, the deeper meaning is that I really don't know what I am talking about. Indeed, I do have a lot to learn about forgiveness, both of others and of myself.

Not surprisingly, forgiveness is a continuous exercise at first. It is a challenge to let go of judgments and negative emotions and forgive someone or yourself. That is exactly why I say it is a continuous process. Asking myself the question "Who am I to judge?" is often a turning point in my practice of forgiveness.

For some time I have been practicing forgiveness every day. Every single day holds at least one exercise for me in forgiveness of someone in my life, someone in my community, someone in my golf league, or someone in the news. I have been, most importantly, practicing forgiving myself for something I have done or not done, for something I have said or not said.

As I learn about forgiveness, I see more clearly why Jesus started His lesson to us by saying, "Judge not, and you shall not be judged."

Most often, the reason I must practice forgiveness is because I have been judgmental or I have not chosen my emotions and let anger or resentment well up inside of me.

As I learn to let go of my deeply ingrained instincts to judge and as I develop a greater capacity to choose my emotions, I am becoming more loving, and I have to forgive less and less often. My prayer of "Lord have mercy" becomes more of a prayer of humility than a prayer asking for forgiveness.

This chapter discusses the lessons I have learned in practicing and experiencing forgiveness. The discussion will focus on the process I have learned from David to help me understand how to forgive others and also how to forgive myself.

For privacy reasons, I will not focus on whom I needed to forgive or what I needed to forgive in myself or others. There is one exception. Perhaps you can guess. I needed to forgive Mom.

***

I met with David for a session on forgiveness following what was a powerful session on anger a few weeks earlier, as discussed in the chapter "Let Go and Take Control." From David's notes and my recollections, here is how the session unfolded.

At the outset David stated, "Forgiveness is a gift we give ourselves." He suggested that my lack of forgiveness might be a huge weight I was carrying, that any energy expended on resentment or anger from the past was only hurting myself. It was not hurting the other people because they had moved on. He added that when I released the weight of not forgiving, I would have a lot more energy.

Hmm ... interesting perspective. I had always focused on weight as a physical attribute, and now it is being presented as a mental attribute as well.

In this session David had me enter a round room and sit down on one of the two straight-back chairs that were in the center of the room. David explained, "The other chair is the 'listening chair.' Whomever we put in that other chair cannot get up, speak, or do anything unless you or I give him or her permission to do so. When that person leaves the round room, he or she won't remember anything." I would always be safe.

David instructed me, "On the count of three, the one person who caused you more pain, more tears, and more frustration than anyone else from the very beginning of your life will be in that chair. One, two, three. Who goes in that chair?"

My mother was in the listening chair. David guided me to tell my mother how she had hurt me and how she had made me feel. I began to confront Mom.

> You hurt me when you hit me with the books.
> You made me feel like a bad girl.
> You made me feel like you didn't love me.
> You made me feel very angry with you.
> You made me think of how to get back at you.
> All I really wanted was for you to be proud of me and
>   love me.
> But you always found something I did wrong.
> You seemed to care more about the other kids than me.

David asked me where I felt the anger in my body. "In my stomach," I answered. My stomach was in knots. My head hurt. It was throbbing. My left knee was aching. Tears were streaming down my face. I felt my anger throughout my body, and my angry emotions overflowed into tears.

The next step in the process was very important. David said, "Follow my instructions immediately and instantly. Three, two, one. You are in the other chair. You are your mother, Eileen."

With all of the ammunition I had just given him, David confronted my mother, which was actually me, in the listening chair. I was seeing the situation through my mother's eyes.

David gently asked the tough and honest questions:

> Eileen, what is wrong with you? *I lost it.*
>
> Did you want to make her feel that way? *No.*
>
> Did you want to hurt her like that? *No.*
>
> Did you know she felt that you didn't love her? *No.*
>
> Did you know that she thought you cared more about
> her brothers and sisters than her? *No.*
>
> Do you love her? *Yes.*
>
> Are you proud of her? *Yes.*
>
> If you knew back then what you know now, would you
> have done things differently? *Yes.*

As my mother, I said, "I lost it. It was a very long day. I was so angry. Little Alison was manipulating her older sister, and she had lied to me."

Hmm. I realized I did play games and thought I could get away with it. Mom called me out.

As my mother, I was sad. "I was not thinking about what Alison was feeling. She is a big challenge for me. I did not really think I was hurting her, certainly not physically."

It was true. Mom did not really hurt me, and I realized I continued to be manipulative by getting up and faking a limp. "Of course, I am proud of her. Of course, I love her. In the moment my emotions got the better of the loving, good mother inside of me. I wish I could take it all back."

David continued to talk to me as my mother, Eileen.

Eileen, you have hurt Alison. You have let her down, and there is nothing you can do about it. It is all water under the bridge. What if there was something you could do to undo the damage from this moment on and give her back her life, would you be interested? *Yes.* It will take a gift of love. Are you still interested? *Yes.*

You won't have the control. Alison will have all the control and the final decision. Are you still interested? *Yes.*

Good. This is what you need to do. You need to ask Alison to forgive you for everything you ever did that hurt her. If you do that, then she becomes free, and the damage is undone. It is a gift of love because you do not get to benefit from it at all. When you leave this round room you will forget that this has even taken place, and Alison will be free. Would you like to do that? *Yes.*

Ask Alison to forgive you for everything you ever did that hurt her, and be specific!

So Mom talked to me and told me all the things I always wanted to hear. "I am so sorry I hurt you. I really am very proud of you. I truly do love you, more deeply than you know. You are precious to me."

Time out. This all really happened. This is actually what I said and what I said as my mother as the forgiveness session progressed. As I write this, I am smiling because I know it to be true, and it is profound. I realized Mom loved me. She knew me and saw through me. She was the disciplinarian in the family. She was teaching me a lesson. Mom did the very best she could. She was a loving and caring mother.

The session continued to the denouement. Would I choose to forgive my dear mother? I was back to grown-up Alison. In the same gentle and firm voice David had used when he talked to Mom, he said,

> Well, Alison, it has all come down to forgiveness. If you
> decide to forgive your mother, who has hurt you, you
> become free, free from all the hurt, and she can never
> affect you the same way again. You get your life back.
> Let me tell you what I mean by forgiveness. First of
> all, forgiveness does not mean you condone what
> happened. It does not mean that you like who hurt
> you. It does not mean that you forget. Forgiveness is a
> change that happens inside of you, that frees you from
> the past. Would you like that? *Yes.*
>
> Do you want to forgive your mother and set yourself
> free? *Yes.*
>
> Good. This is how you will do it. I am about to become
> quiet. Then you start talking and keep talking until
> all the anger from the past is gone. When it is gone,
> then the forgiveness is complete. Begin. I forgive you
> because ...

Finally, still in a trance, from my heart, I said the following:

> Mom, I forgive you because I know you loved me.
> I forgive you because I know you were doing the best
> you could.

> I forgive you because I know it was not easy. We were poor.
> I forgive you because I know I was not an easy child for you, because I played manipulative games.
> I forgive you because I know you always wanted to be loved just as you loved all of us.
> Mom, I forgive you.

David brought me back to my feelings and asked, "How does your stomach feel now?" This was important because my stomach had been upset before, but now it was calm and quiet. My head had stopped throbbing. My knee was not aching.

In this final phase of my session on forgiveness, David guided me.

> Now you have learned about how good it is to forgive.
> Would you like to take advantage of this power that you
> have right now? There are others who have hurt you.
> Would you like to forgive all these people, be it family,
> friends, or business associates, and truly set yourself
> free from the past?

In my subconscious mind, as David was quiet, I silently named and said every person who had ever hurt me. One by one, I snipped the ties that bound me to my anger, which was long past, and set myself free. Hmm. This took a little while.

As I came out of my trance, fully awake and aware, I felt spent, but in a good way. This had been a profound and deeply cathartic session. I was feeling a sense of awe. I felt lighter. David asked me to finish the two key sentences with the first thought that came to mind. I have changed because:

> Now I *Know* ... forgiveness.
> Now I *Feel* ... I truly love myself.

There it was again—knowing forgiveness and feeling love.

And then spontaneously, I added, "I feel splendiferous!"

We laughed. David asked, "Is *splendiferous* a real word?" I believe splendiferous is a real word, and it is now my word for my world.

Mother loved all five of us. She loved children. Mom did everything for us. Mom was a full-time caregiver all of her life. I can only begin to appreciate the demands of raising five children on a shoestring budget, even making most of our clothes. I was smart and a smart-aleck handful, maybe even a little manipulative way back then. Mom did the very best she could, and she was caring and loving and supportive of all of us. Did I support her in return? Not so much in my early years. In my later years, particularly after my brother's untimely passing, I was much more attentive. However, I was still judgmental.

Many mother-daughter relationships are complex. This chapter is my opportunity, through my tears and my smiles, to ask out loud, "Mom, I hope you will forgive me." Somehow I now know she does.

Flashback: It was a summer day in August almost eighteen years earlier. Mom and Dad were visiting Doug and me at our lake house. Mom and I had spent the morning gardening and shopping and took a break for lunch. We were at the local country club, sitting on the porch, having lunch, marveling at the lake and the beauty of nature. We both said, "Isn't life good?"

Mom got up and went to a small child playing by the sea wall. She was a little concerned that he was not closely supervised, and she picked up an interesting rock to distract and to engage the little boy. They were deep in conversation for some time, and then the father of the boy appeared.

Mom returned to sit with me and said, "I love little children." This was particularly poignant because not one of her five children had had children of their own. At that moment I realized she had no grandchildren. That was probably one of her fondest dreams. She never said a word to me about not having grandchildren. She never pried or complained.

The next morning, Sunday, Mom was not feeling well. Mom and Dad left to see my older sister and then returned to their home in upstate New York. On Monday morning I was at my desk in Chicago on a conference call to a colleague in London, and I took an urgent message from my brother, who said, "Mom is dead." Mom had died suddenly in her sleep that night from a ruptured spleen, presumably caused by a virus that had turned deadly.

I never had a chance to say this to Mom directly. "Mom, I love you. I forgive you. Please forgive me."

As I tell this story and wipe away my tears, I remember the important lessons David has taught me. Anger comes from within the person, from within me. I am not responsible for another person's emotions, only my own. I can choose to react to another person's emotions, or I can choose my emotions. I could have just said to Mom, "I am so sorry," when I was five years old. Instead I carried that baggage around for years and years.

Now after all these years, I have released the pain and the guilt. Forgiving does indeed release a huge weight, and I do feel splendiferous.

***

Several months passed since my session with David on forgiveness of others. I believed it was time to focus on forgiving myself. There was a nagging doubt deep within that I may have some unfinished work to do on me. I was starting to listen to my inner voice. I was starting to be more honest with myself.

I knew I had some unfinished business with forgiving myself.

I talked with David for reassurance. As the session evolved, I wanted the option to stay within and to silently say the things I wanted and needed to say to myself. As usual, David was accommodating, stipulating only that my decision take place in the moment so that it would be both a conscious and subconscious decision on how the session proceeded.

Once I was fully relaxed and in trance, David guided me to the "forgiveness room," as I call it, and I put myself in the chair. David was asking me to go back to that part of me that had been hurting the most. Indeed, I did know exactly where I was going. In my college days, I made a very bad error in judgment. I did not and will not share this with David or anyone. It is something only I know. I'm sorry to appear so mysterious. It is just something so private that it is only between me and my Higher Power, God.

David was guiding me to reflect on the event and to accept and forgive myself. I was not ready. The tears were streaming down my face. David was coaching me, and the dialogue between us flowed.

> Did you hurt anyone? *No, just myself.*
>
> Were you young? *Yes, I was very young.*
>
> Did you know better? *Yes, I knew it was wrong.*
>
> So you made a mistake. *Yes, I made a terrible mistake.*
>
> So you were young and made a mistake.
>
> Will you ever do that again? *No. Never.*

I continued my conversation in private between just me and God. Finally, I felt the forgiveness. God had forgiven me. A feeling of amazing peace and grace washed over my entire body. Then I was able to forgive myself.

I felt the love and the very deep tie between love and forgiveness. How could I possibly describe the feeling, the experience of totally, completely, unconditionally forgiving myself? How does one describe a glorious sunrise? Awe. I was in a deeply thankful and reverent state of awe.

As I was coming out of my trance, David asked me to finish the two key sentences with the first thought that came to mind.

> I have changed because now I *Know* … I can trust
> myself and experience deeper joy.
>
> I have changed because now I *Feel* … more at peace
> with myself.

Trusting myself, experiencing a deeper sense of joy, and feeling more at peace in my mind and my soul, I could see that every session was leading to deeper and deeper self-realizations.

This was another long and deeply cathartic session for me. I left David's office more at peace with myself and loving myself at a deeper level.

***

I had learned so much in this session on forgiveness. Indeed, a huge weight had been released yet again. In my morning readings, the messages of forgiveness in the Holy Bible and *A Course in Miracles* just jumped off the page. David explained that this was the subconscious mind at work. My experience of forgiveness in our session was opening my mind to see and feel forgiveness in everything I read and everywhere I went.

I would like to share some of the most impactful words of wisdom from a few key resources. I hope as you reflect on these excerpts that you will understand the enormous power of forgiveness and how it is so intricately related to choosing emotions and to the power of love.

The teachings of Jesus of Nazareth as told in the Gospels are shining lights of the spiritual importance of forgiveness. This chapter heading includes my favorite saying of Jesus from the Gospel According to Luke. Here are a few more quotes from the Gospel According to Luke and the Gospel According to Matthew.

- "When he saw their faith, he said, 'Friend, your sins are forgiven you.' Which is easier to say, 'Your sins are forgiven you' or say, "Stand up and walk"?'" (Luke 5:20–23).

91

- "Give us each day our daily bread. And forgive us our sins, for we ourselves forgive everyone indebted to us" (Luke 11:3–4, The Lord's Prayer).

- "For everyone who asks receives, and everyone who searches finds, and for everyone who knocks, the door will be opened" (Luke: 11:10).

- "Then the father said to him, 'Son, you are always with me, and all that is mine is yours. But we had to celebrate and rejoice, because this brother of yours was dead and has come to life; he was lost and has been found'" (Luke: 15:31–32). The Parable of the Prodigal Son and His Brother is one of the best-known acts of forgiveness.

- "Then Peter came and said to him, 'Lord, if another member of the church sins against me, how often should I forgive? As many as seven times?' Jesus said to him, 'Not seven times, but I tell you, seventy-seven times'" (Matthew 18:21–22).

- "Father, forgive them; for they do not know what they are doing" (Luke 23:34).

There are also powerful sayings from *A Course in Miracles*.

- "Forgiveness is the key to happiness. Here is the answer to your search for peace. The unforgiving mind is full of fear, and offers no room to be itself. The unforgiving mind is sad, without the hope of respite and release from pain" (Workbook for Students, lesson 121).

- "What could you want forgiveness cannot give? Do you want peace? Forgiveness offers it. Do you want happiness, a quiet mind, a certainty of purpose, and a sense of worth and beauty that transcend the world? Do you want care and safety, and the warmth of sure protection always? ... All this forgiveness offers you, and more. It sparkles on your eyes as you awake, and gives you joy with which to meet the day" (Workbook for Students, lesson 122).

- "Each lily of forgiveness offers all the world the silent miracle of love" (Workbook for Students, section 13, lesson 340/341).

All of these words of wisdom were written in my journal. I was meditating on forgiveness a lot. In fact, there was a three-month stretch where forgiveness was my key focal point at least four to five times a week.

Some of the journal entries from my meditations include the following:

Ali: Meditating on forgiveness of others. I am thinking of very specific people, times and places. One by one, I forgive. I forgive wholly, totally, completely, with no ambiguity, with no hesitation, without any doubt. I let go of all resentment and grievances ... I forgive ... I heal ... I am at peace.

Ali: I am focused on forgiveness this morning. My knee and left leg are throbbing. Is that Mom hitting me? I persevere. I have a higher sense of forgiveness with God in the picture. I think of my session on forgiveness of self and my private thoughts. I tear up. And ... a sense of calm ... my leg does not hurt.

Ali: Once I forgive myself, truly, I am free to forgive everyone.

Ali: I accept myself and all my past. I forgive myself. I can be at One with myself. I am one Self.

Ali: I am reading *Miracles*. "Forgiveness is its single aim, at which all learning converges." I am overcome with joy. "It is indeed enough." I have come a long way on the journey that started out as a simple summer of renewal.

I hope I am connecting with you and on a deep level, sharing the sense of freedom and joy and love that is the power of forgiveness.

***

I have been writing a lot about the past. It is time to turn our attention to the present. Isn't it a little ridiculous? Oops, wrong word. Let me start over. Isn't there a better way to move forward such that forgiveness is not something I need to do every day?

Yes, I am starting to learn there is a better way. This is the intersection of learning about forgiveness with learning to choose my emotions, learning to let go of expectations, and learning to be a lot less judgmental.

First, look back to the chapter titled "Let Go and Take Control," when I was in trance and talking to my mom. Reread what I was saying. "You hurt me. You made me angry. You made me feel like a bad girl." All these phrases made it clear that I was handing my emotional control over to someone else. Turn it around to "Emotions are choices."

Does this mean that I have had a lobotomy and no longer feel angry? No, of course not. What it means is that whenever I do get angry and there are some red flags that I now recognize when I am getting angry, I pause for a minute. I step back and observe the situation and myself. Did my ego come to the forefront? Was the other person treating me unfairly? What's the point in getting angry? I am only hurting myself. Taking deep breaths is always helpful at these junctures. Sometimes I can pause and regroup in the moment. Sometimes it takes me hours or even days to regroup.

As I continue to improve in my ability to live by this mantra, I can better decide how I feel. I realize that I cannot control anyone else's feelings, only my own. It is a much calmer and more peaceful and loving way to live.

One of David's texts reinforced exactly this point. This was as part of a dialogue during which I was regrouping after wrestling with my emotions. David texted, "There is only one question to ask yourself. Am I choosing love or fear? They cannot coexist. Let go of trying to control or feeling responsible for other people's emotions, and choose yours. In the NOW, the only place you truly exist. Namaste."

Second, I examine the role of my expectations and the interplay of choosing my emotions and forgiveness. Expectations are a measuring rod, how I expect other people to be or to treat me. It may be as simple as being on time for a meeting. So when a person is late, why do I take that as a signal of disrespect or disregard for me? Well, for starters, I was taught that at home and in my business dealings, my time is important and that I am important. Do you see the ego in those thoughts and the underlying emotions? Accept what is happening. Does this mean I don't take action? No. Rather it means that I first let go of my ego and accept the situation. If I cannot change the past, why am I trying to change the present moment? Only then do I take action. As David has said to me on many occasions, "Expectations are preconceived disappointments."

Third, I learned to be less judgmental, to focus on suspending judgment. I practiced recognizing, observing, and redirecting all my explicit and implicit judgmental thoughts and actions. Do you notice now why I changed the word *ridiculous* and took another approach in the opening paragraph of this section? If I am going to get rid of the *shoulds* in my life, I need to get rid of the *shoulds* in all of my relationships. In *Inner Wisdom*, Louise Hay writes, "'Should' is a word that makes a prisoner of me. Every time I say 'should,' I am making myself wrong, or I am making someone else wrong. From here on in, I replace the word 'should' with the word 'could.' 'Could' lets me know I have choice, and choice is freedom. I always have choice."

The key lesson is that when I simply accept, when I do not judge others or myself, when I give goodness, peace, and trust, there is nothing to forgive, and I am free!

I readily admit I am a work in progress. There are some lessons I need to learn over and over again. At least now I know where to go in my mind to regroup and to move on.

Ali's List of Changes and Choices

The list of changes and choices is a little smaller than the one in the last chapter. No matter. These steps are huge. Besides, who is judging anyhow?

1. I started increasing my use of the word *splendiferous*. This is *my* word, my world!

2. I started eliminating the phrase "you make me ... sad, angry or happy." "You make me" is the signal that I have given emotional control over to someone else. No one can hurt me. Only I can hurt myself. In meditation one morning, I ask, "Why does love hurt?" Unconditional love cannot hurt. Then I realize I had some unmet expectations that I had inadvertently and in error attached to love.

3. I started eliminating the word *should*. The word *could* puts judgment to the side and opens the mind to the freedom of choice.

4. I started forgiving myself and everyone.

5. I started reading voraciously. For years, I had only read business books on leadership and management to keep up-to-date with the latest research and developments in the field of security analysis and portfolio management and asset allocation. Occasionally, for plane trips I would pick up paperbacks, always a mystery or an adventure or a spy novel, just for escape and fun.

   a. The floodgates of my inquiring mind open. I read *The Secret Language of Feelings* by Calvin D. Banyan. I have discovered Louise Hay. I am a late bloomer. Eckhart Tolle's *The Power of Now* was another new treasure. I have so much catching up to do.

   b. Hafiz, one of the great Sufi poets, entered the picture, thanks again to David. I certainly never heard Hafiz quoted on Wall Street. At his essence, Hafiz lives by loving and knowing the loving God. Rapture! I found *Love Poems from God: Twelve Voices from the East and West* by Daniel Ladinsky and read the great spiritual teachings and poems by people of faith across many centuries and religions.

c. I read the Bible, specifically the book of Proverbs, the book of Psalms, and the entire New Testament.

d. I would open at random to a page in *Inner Wisdom: Meditations for the Heart and Soul* by Louise L. Hay.

At one point, I started a list of all the books I am reading, and I kept adding to the list. When that list grew to more than a hundred references, I decided to stop counting. After all, many people have passed this way before. I decided to select only the readings that I found to be most impactful to me on my journey. The selected list of readings is included in Resources after the Appendix.

6. I chose love and let go of anger and resentment.

Gratitude. Silence. Music. Reading. Learning. Religion. Spirituality. All these practices are now part of the way I start my day and how I started to live a new life.

CHAPTER 8
Release and Rejoice

Without fear, we are able to see more clearly
our connections to others.
Without fear, we have more room
for understanding and compassion.
Without fear, we are truly free.

—Thich Nhat Hanh

At the outset David and I discussed why it made sense for me to commit to a session specifically on fear. It was a natural outgrowth of the tremendous release I had experienced from my sessions on letting go of anger and then forgiving others and myself. I could feel the release, both physically and emotionally.

David explained that fear has many disguises and is actually the root cause behind many other negative emotions, including anger, worry, anxiety, guilt, frustration, depression, inadequacy, jealousy, and more. We are not talking about the kind of fear when a person's life is in imminent danger. Rather it may be fear of the unknown; fear of failure; fear of being hurt, either mentally or emotionally; fear of loss; fear of missing something, someone, or some personal attribute; fear of the death of a loved one; or fear of your own death.

I realized by committing to explore and resolve the emotions of fear, I was going deeper and deeper within. Who knew what I would learn next?

As I will reveal later in this chapter, I discovered, much to my surprise, that I had lived my whole life in fear.

It is important to specifically acknowledge that the focus was on releasing fear. This did not mean denying fear, repressing fear, or laughing in the face of fear and pushing through fear. Rather the primary purpose was to understand the root causes of my fears, to accept and acknowledge my fears, and then to let go of and release my fears.

Indeed, fear had been a major force in shaping my personality and worldview. My fear on 9/11 was a key driver in my emotional response and major changes in my life choices. Fear was the driver in the summer of 2009 when I realized I could and inevitably would lose everyone important in my life. In retrospect, it is now clear the reason I chose that day in May was to deal with my repressed fears. Fear was a major catalyst that ultimately led me to make positive changes in my life.

I felt that fear—primal, dark, empty, and hopeless. Just a few months before I was reeling, I was desperate. I made my first appointment with David and focused on the obvious surface issues of weight loss and stress. Then we moved on to letting go of anger and experiencing how to truly forgive others and myself. I was ready to move on to the underlying issue of my fears.

Could I have started my journey with fear, and short-circuited the process as I would typically want to do? You know the type—the "Let's cut to the chase" and "What's the bottom line?" people. With honesty and humility, I could not and would not have started this journey if I had been asked to start with the root causes of my emotional issues, my fears. This is a great example of the *art* in the design and orchestration of David's process, The Best Me NOW!

My session with David on fear took place about three months into my journey. The impact was instantaneous. At the same time, the levels of fear, the kinds of fear, and relearning how to release fear all evolved over the course of the next year and continue to evolve. That is my perspective and testament to my growth.

This chapter is titled "Release and Rejoice." It does not include the word *fear* because the key word is *release*. That is the lesson. The opening quote from Thich Nhat Hanh, a revered Vietnamese Zen Buddhist monk, teacher, author, poet, and peace activist, expresses very beautifully the purpose of releasing fear. Releasing fear takes down walls and allows me to feel more connected. It also frees up my energy to be more compassionate and loving, to be happier.

After this important session with David on fear, I truly released the root cause of my fears and rejoiced.

***

In July, I had a session with David during which we focused on fear. The purpose was to trace back my emotional history through my subconscious mind to recall the root cause of my fears.

In our discussion beforehand, I talked about my fears. I remembered my early childhood fear of bridges, including the Whitestone Bridge, where I closed my eyes and imagined that the car was traveling up the suspension cables and we were launched into space. I also had a recurring early childhood nightmare of a pirate—I could see the big hat and the cruel eyebrows—breaking through a basement bedroom window. I remembered stories from my mother of how I was afraid of the sand and would not venture away from the blanket at Jones Beach. I also talked about my fear of cars and driving and speed.

I realized that fear was an issue in my life and that I had never focused on the emotion of fear in the past. It was way too scary. In fact, I had consciously avoided addressing my fear, as many people do, because I didn't think I could control it.

David reminded me that all of our emotions reside in the subconscious mind, which is organized by emotion. He explained that each emotion we experience is connected in our memory to every time we experience that emotion. It is like a string of beads. He explained that in hypnosis we could follow that feeling of fear back to its origin and release it.

In my session David guided me back to when I first felt fear. Initially, I was on familiar territory—fear of high bridges like the Whitestone Bridge and the childhood nightmare of the pirate breaking into my bedroom through the basement window. David continued to guide me further and further back in time.

And then ... Where was I? Where was I?

David asked me, "Alison, where are you? What are you feeling?"

I didn't know where I was. From seemingly nowhere, from deep in my subconscious mind, I had a profound realization. I was in my mother's womb, and I was about to be birthed. I was very afraid. I was terrified.

Stop! Time out. How could this be? Had I really gone back to the womb? After the session David explained that the scientific and medical communities have proven that our memories start long before we are born, and even though we may not remember them consciously, they are stored in the subconscious mind. This is why many expectant parents play music and even talk to their babies in the womb.

In my trance I felt the fear. I did not want to be born. I was afraid. Mom was horribly afraid. I felt it in my body.

David guided me as grown-up Alison to talk to little Alison. David said, "Grown-up Alison, tell little Alison where she is and what is happening, and tell her what she needs to know for her to get through this without being afraid. Let her know the outcome."

As grown-up Alison, I recalled the stories of my birth that my mom had told me. I was a breech baby, and the delivery was difficult. Forceps were involved. Mom did not give a lot of details. Perhaps it was too painful a memory. I was thinking about the bruises and the damages to my skull, all the things I had imagined from the story I had been told. As grown-up Alison, I was still in fear, and I did not yet know how to coach little Alison to let her know that she was going to be okay. David continued to coach me to focus on the outcome and how to reassure little Alison that everything would be all right. So I told little Alison, "You will grow up to be a normal child. You will have fun. You will be loved and live a long life. In fact, you will live an amazing life!"

I realized she was going to be okay. I knew I was all right, even better than all right. I saw and felt that everything would be all right for little Alison.

I explained and coached little Alison about what was going on. "You are in your mother's womb. You are about to be born. Everything is going to be okay. Your mom is very afraid. You are turned around the wrong way. You are a breech baby, and the doctors need to turn you around so you come out headfirst. It may not be pretty, but it does not matter because you will be okay. Everything is going to be okay. You are scared because your mother is scared. Mom loves you very much. I know you will be okay. You will grow up. You will go to school, have friends, get married, and travel the world. You will have an absolutely amazing life."

The key message was, "You are loved, and you are always safe and secure."

David was patient and continued to guide the process. "Little Alison, did you hear grown-up Alison? Do you believe her? Are you ready to go through this without being afraid? Hmmm. No, not yet."

Grown-up Alison continued to coach, "Little Ali, you are safe and secure." Hmmm. "You are okay. You are loved. Are you ready to be born?" This continued on for quite some time.

Finally, yes, I was ready. I was born. I heard myself say, "Here I am, world!" with arms outstretched and with joy in my heart. I realized there and then I had lived in fear all of my life.

Then David addressed little Alison. "Little Alison, grown-up Alison came back and taught you that you are going to be okay, that you are safe and you are loved. Now I want you to tell grown-up Alison how you have changed and what you know that is different now."

So Little Alison gave me feedback and said, "I have changed now because I know I am safe. I know I am loved. I know I am never alone."

"Now, tell Alison how you feel," David instructed to little Alison. So little Alison said to me, "Now I feel safe. I am not afraid to be born. I am very excited to be alive!"

David then brought little Alison and grown-up Alison together. "Little Alison, now tell grown-up Alison, 'I have changed, and as I have changed, you have changed because I am you. I live in your heart, where all your feelings come from.'"

Little Alison again coached me. "Alison, I am very happy now. I am smiling and excited. You did a great job! I am not afraid anymore!"

So the cycle of grown-up Alison coaching little Alison and then little Alison coaching grown-up Alison was completed. The string of beads leading me back to my experience in my mother's womb, my primal fear, had now been snipped. As little Alison was released of fear, I released my fear.

As I emerged from hypnosis, David asked me to complete the two key closing sentences. I have changed because:

> Now I *Know* ... I am always with me and I love myself.
> Now I *Feel* ... what total peace feels like.

Aw! I am never alone. I am always with my Self. I was starting to find that deep connection to our Higher Power, the Holy Spirit, the Inner

Self, my God. I am never alone. I am always loved. Where there is love, there is peace and contentment, and there is no fear.

As I continued over the next several months to meditate and reinforce my release of these primal fears, I recalled that my first name, Alison, was not actually on the original hospital birth certificate. My Dad always loved to tell the story that he and Mom could not agree on a name for me. Dad came up with a brilliant idea from a poem he was reading. The poet had a pet goat named Alison, spelled with one "l" rather than two. So the story goes. That is how and why I was named Alison when I arrived home. I will never know the real story. However, I now see this as possible evidence that Mom and Dad were so shaken by the bruising and the deformity of my little body as I was delivered that they truly did not expect me to live.

Had fear been my motivating factor all my life? Had fear been a driving force behind my relentless pursuit of achievement? With my eyes closed to the fear deep inside, I had always plowed full steam ahead. I had to be in control, to keep my fears at bay.

That July day early on in my journey, when we snipped the thread of fear that traced back to the womb, I felt an amazing emotional release. That night my heart was light. That day opened new doors for me to see with new eyes, to experience life with a new heart.

I was afraid to tell anyone about my experience of tracing my deep-rooted fears back to the womb. I was afraid people would think it was too weird, that I had gone over the edge. Some lessons just need to be learned again and again.

As I became more comfortable and confident in sharing a very personal part of my journey with a few close friends, they in turn opened up to me and shared some incredible experiences. Not only was I beginning to change, I was starting to change and improve the relationships with other people in my life as well. This proverbial ripple effect was very real.

Losing Aunt Mary

As I have said, in the summer of 2009, I realized I could and inevitably would lose everyone important in my life. Then where would I be? At that point, I did not even include myself as someone on the list of people important in my life.

Many people have dealt with similar issues and even more challenging life and death issues. Why couldn't I deal with these events? Everyone survived, right? Read on.

For twenty years I had believed it was my purpose in life to care for my dear Aunt Mary. The oldest of seven children on my mother's side, Mary had always been a role model for me. Mary was an Assistant Vice President and an officer in a bank in New York City. In an era when women were not accepted in professional roles, she was the banker to many of the top people in the garment district. Mary was glamorous and had an amazing sense of style. She had a remarkable talent for reading and understanding people. Mary was my other mother. We had a deep bond and mutual admiration for each other. Once she moved to Ohio, I visited with Mary almost every day. Through all the moves, four in total over seven years, I had somehow managed to help her keep her beautiful cat, Boy, with her as she approached her ninety-fifth birthday.

How would I possibly cope with the inevitable loss of Mary? How could I deal with the fact I was losing a little of Mary every day as her progressive dementia, most likely Alzheimer's, continued on its inevitable path? I felt I would have no purpose after Mary passed on.

In my mind, Alzheimer's is a tragic disease. One day I said to David, "It is a terrible thing to lose one's mind. It is a terrible thing to watch someone so dear to you lose her mind. It is a tragedy to lose a little bit of a person you love so dearly, little by little every single day."

David suggested a different perspective. "It is only Mary's mind that is going. Mary's soul, her essence, is as beautiful as it always was and always will be." Hmmm …

After this conversation with David, I turned to one of my favorite quotes from *The Messiah's Handbook: Reminders for the Advanced Soul*, which was written by Jonathan Bach.

> *The mark of your ignorance is the depth of your belief in justice and tragedy. What the caterpillar calls the end of the world, the master calls a butterfly.*

This quote has stuck with me from the day I read the book. The final sentence is beautiful. The first sentence, however, I did not understand.

What was wrong with justice? I was pondering my ignorance. Then it came to me. Nothing was wrong with justice, except judgment. Judgment is not peace. It is not trust. It is fear. What was tragedy? It also was judgment and fear. I have a little more insight into the meaning behind the first sentence.

However, I continued to persist, as is my nature, and continued my conversation with David, saying, "I still believe that Mary or anyone losing their mind is a tragedy." Privately, I also feared that one day I might suffer from the same affliction.

David observed, "Mary's body and mind are not who she is. Mary's spirit and soul are the same as they ever were and always will be. Your memories of Mary, your experiences of Mary, are always with you. They will never leave you, so Mary will always be with you."

It was only then I realized that my memories of Mary would always be with me. My experience with Mary is truly eternal. Aha! I experienced the beauty and the peace in releasing my fear of losing Aunt Mary.

In my meditations and spiritual journey, I continued to work on the issues of fear and loss.

Several months later I wrote in my journal, "I transform my prayer for Mary from 'Please, God, don't let Mary suffer' to 'I offer God's peace and love to Mary in the here and now and in the hereafter.'"

I also found an even deeper sense of peace. This peace was something I shared with Mary every day. Releasing fear allowed me to transform my prayers for Mary from worry and anxiety over suffering to trusting God and feeling the transforming energy of peace and love.

A few weeks later, after sharing a pre-Christmas dinner at the assisted living dining room with Mary and two of my good friends, I wrote,

> Thank you, my friends, for lunch with Mary and me. It
> means a lot to me. I am sure you could see the pain on
> my face at times. Please know that I am coming to peace

with what is. Mary and God are teaching me a lot about
acceptance, trust, patience, staying in the moment, and
being at one with loss. As I lose a little bit of Mary every
day, I now find peace in knowing that I will never lose
Mary. She will always be with me. This I Know.

A couple of weeks later, I wrote to these same friends and said that
I often told Mary that she was on God's time. I always intended that
prayer to calm her fears about what and why this was happening to
her. With my meditations on loss and releasing, I realized that it was
actually me that was learning to accept that Mary was on God's time.
One friend wrote back, "Letting go is really difficult. It is a huge step
forward in one's spiritual development."

I made a lot of progress on my journey, most especially with loving
Mary in the moment and rejoicing in the good days. Mary's love was
amazing. Mary often said, "You are my angel," and, "You do not know
how much I love you." There were times when Mary looked out of the
window and said, "Thank God for the blue sky today." How special
was that?

Then Mary started to suddenly and swiftly wind down. Mary lost
twenty pounds. She slept most of the day and was barely eating or
taking fluids. I learned that I still had a lot to learn about releasing loved
ones and allowing them to pass on.

I came face-to-face with the realization I might not be holding Mary's
hand when she passed. I did not consciously think about this picture.
However, it was there in my subconscious. I so wanted to be there. I
wanted to make sure Mary knew she was not alone. As I looked within,
I realized that Mary was never alone. God was always with her. What

was it that made me feel my holding her hand would really make a difference to her? Yes, it would make a difference to me perhaps. However, this was just fear creeping into my thoughts and emotions. I was not in control of exactly when Mary would pass and where she would be and where I would be. I needed to choose love, not fear.

The second realization for me was that I could not control how Mary passed. Of course not. How silly. However, I was initially tied up in knots, making sure that Mary was getting enough fluids, that she would not become dehydrated and require an IV or a trip to the ER, which I knew Mary would not want. As I sprang into action, talked with the nursing staff, and engaged hospice, I realized I was doing what was important to make sure Mary was not neglected. How Mary passed was outside of my control.

For almost four years, I had cared for Mary and for her cat, Boy. I visited with her, checked in on her, took her for walks in the wheel chair or out for a ride when it was possible, fed the cat, and fed the birds almost every day. Ahh, deeper and deeper, getting to layers of guilt—I could not ever do enough—and fear. So Mary gave me yet another opportunity to go deeper and truly understand that I am not in control. Mary was on God's time. I had yet another opportunity to learn to release my deepest fears and rejoice in the moments we shared together. Mary lived on. Apparently, she had more lessons to teach me.

At that point in my journey, I reflected that God and Mary gave me a test, and I joked with close friends and said, "I flunked!" That was a little of my New York humor. My dad's humor is always there.

David coached me, "Did you flunk? Or did you just need to learn and reflect on a deeper level what it truly means to release a loved one?" It was the difference between judging and not judging.

In closing, the reason this chapter is not titled "fear" is because the focus is on releasing.

Where there is love, fear cannot exist. Rejoice!

Ali's Changes and Choices

It is at this juncture in my journey that I started to integrate and expand my readings with the work I had been doing with David on both forgiveness and letting go of fear.

1. David introduced me to the *Tao Te Ching: A New English Version* by Stephen Mitchell. I discovered Dr. Wayne Dyer's book *Change Your Thoughts, Change Your Mind, Living the Wisdom of the Tao* and five other online renditions of the Tao. I read the Tao and the Bible every day.

2. David also introduced me to "The Ten Characteristics of God's Teachers," a section of the book *A Course in Miracles*. Wow! This was all new to me. I was so intrigued that I bought *The Combined Volume, A Course in Miracles* and started the Workshop for Students by doing one lesson a day in my morning quiet time. David also introduced me to Richard Bach's *Illusions: The Adventures of a Reluctant Messiah*. This was just the start.

3. My faith started to blossom. In the silence I started to understand the way as Jesus and Lao Tzu had taught.

4. I was letting go. I was not clinging. Learning to let go of dear Aunt Mary, of my beloved chocolate lab, Zacharia, and of a terrific board experience.

5. I was choosing love, not fear.

I was walking. Maybe I was learning how to fly!

CHAPTER 9

Look Within and Love Me

It is not how much we do,
but how much love is put into the doing.
It is not how much we give,
but how much love is put into the giving.

—Mother Teresa

Let's pause. We have covered a lot of ground so far. In Part 2, "Opening New Doors of My Mind," I learned that I could choose my emotions. I do not have to react. My emotions are my choice. Then I learned to let go of anger, resentment, and expectations and to take control. The next step in the process naturally flowed into learning how to forgive everyone and most importantly, myself. As we moved on to addressing my longstanding and deeply rooted fears, I was feeling a new sense of freedom and joy. This was very exciting and energizing.

All of the steps in the process to this point have been about jettisoning the baggage, old habits, and behaviors that were literally weighing me down. Another way to say it is that I had held myself hostage for much of my adult life with an array of negative emotions and limiting beliefs.

David's process reflected a key insight. Many people, myself included, need to clean out the closets and recesses of our minds before we can go shopping and looking for what we truly want in our lives.

Does this mean I have perfectly learned all these lessons? No. Sometimes I have the capacity and awareness to instantly recognize a negative emotion, step aside, and adjust accordingly. Sometimes it may take me hours to process and adjust. Sometimes I have to learn the lesson over and over again. Sometimes it is not pretty, meaning that I am very disappointed in myself. My journey is not a straight line, and, importantly, my goal is not about achieving perfection. My objective is to keep walking, to keep learning and moving on to higher and higher levels of awareness, at least until I backslide. Then I must pause, reflect, forgive, and recommit to change and to controlling my emotions. Then I start all over again.

Going Deeply Within

I was prepared to move to a more advanced level in order to open my mind and to open my heart to love. This was another important juncture in my journey. My instinct, which I was starting to trust more and more, was calling me to a spiritual dimension on my journey. This was a personal decision. Each of us continues our journey on our own unique path. I hope you will read on and keep an open mind.

Going within meant that I was starting to understand that happiness was not something found in anything outside of myself, not in my family, my friends, my job, or my house. *Going within* was the start of my journey to find and connect with my inner Self, and I also think of this as the start of my spiritual journey. I usually will capitalize the "S" when I write inner *Self* or *mySelf* to show the respect and the reverence I hold for the spiritual element, the divinity that I personally believe is there in all of us. For me, a spiritual journey is an expansive and inclusive concept. I fully respect everyone's personal religious and spiritual beliefs (or lack of beliefs). My intent is simply to share my experiences. There is no attempt to persuade or judge. Take it for what and how it may speak to you.

This is an opportune juncture in my journey to examine the interplay of time with the metaphor of the labyrinth. Time, as David has discussed with me, has both a horizontal and a vertical dimension. I have lived most of my life in the horizontal dimension of time, the X axis, for the mathematicians out there. There are twenty-four hours in a day, seven days in a week, and fifty-two weeks in a year. For my entire business career, I had thought there was never enough time to do everything on both my professional and my personal to-do lists. As I enter the walking mediation of the labyrinth, I focus on one emotion at a time. When I start the path of the labyrinth and focus on fear, I reflect on each different type of fear. As I move on in my meditations, I work on forgiving one person at a time.

In the vertical dimension of time (or the Y axis), I was entering the spiritual dimension, where body, space, and time do not exist. In the spiritual journey, time is infinite, boundless, and eternal. In the spiritual journey within, there are no limits. Anything is possible.

The journey to my inner *Self* and to the center of the labyrinth was for me a profoundly spiritual experience.

My colloquial term for this next phase of my journey is "To the moon, baby!" The great Sufi poet Hafiz is more eloquent.

What is this precious love and laughter
budding in our hearts?
It is the glorious sound
of a soul waking up!

However you may want to say it, this is exactly where I was in my journey as we move on to the two final chapters of Part 2: "Opening New Doors of My Mind," which provide some insights into my experiences in learning about unconditional love and the oneness of the universe. I call it my spiritual journey. You may label it something entirely different. Frankly, I am not so much into labels. I am into the experience of the journey. I invite you to continue to walk a ways with me.

***

There were several important elements in my mosaic of looking within. I use the word *mosaic* because it brings to mind pieces of a puzzle. The pieces are all different shapes and colors. The boundaries are yet to be defined. In my experience, as a mosaic is crafted and unfolds, it sparkles. I had used this analogy throughout my career as an analyst. I would paint pictures of a company's competitive business strategy or create scenarios of comparative relative performance of global asset classes.

Creating a mosaic of looking within places me as the artist. Indeed, each of us is the artist, the cocreator of our unique mosaic. For me, these steps are not linear. It is not a paint-by-numbers approach, following steps one through three. Rather the pieces of the mosaic come on different days, even in different months. I circle back and fill in more of the picture around the tiles I placed before. I assimilate and integrate, and the patterns and revelations start to emerge. This is a highly individual and creative process for me. Yet the framework is there for every individual to tailor to his or her unique life situation and personal beliefs.

With David, I started a new series of sessions focused on accessing my Higher Power.

In our pre-talk, I shared with David that I would like to specifically focus on staying in the Now, letting go of worrying about the past and the future. In the Now is where I know I find a greater sense of peace and happiness.

David guided me into a very deep trance and instructed me that as my body continued to go deeper and deeper, becoming more and more relaxed, my mind would do something a little bit different. My mind would separate from my body and begin rising and lifting higher and higher. He guided my mind up through a beautiful tunnel that led to higher levels of awareness so that I could connect with my Higher Power and all that I needed or wanted to know. David then became silent and allowed me to privately receive the information from my Higher Power.

As I recall this session, my hands were clasped above my head in prayer. I rose up to the clouds, swirling and twirling. I had no fear. I was feeling deeply loved. In my own mind, I prayed, "Please show me the Way to stay in the present moment, accept, and be grateful for what is." I was receiving messages like, "Stop worrying about what other people think or want you to do. Just be yourself. Trust yourself."

Hmm ... I just needed to be me. I also recall a gentle observation that I appear to have a high regard of myself and a low regard for others. Hmm ... I don't need to build myself up or put other people down. Who do I need to impress? God, my Higher Power, was gently reminding me to care for others less fortunate than me. There were no tears in this session. I felt very light with a profound sense of peace above all the cares *down below*.

When I emerged from this session, David asked me to complete the now familiar two key personal statements that often helped me crystallize my lessons while they were still very fresh in my mind. I have changed because:

> Now I *Know* ... I can see the light.
> Now I *Feel* ... a deeper sense of letting go and a deeper
> sense of peace.

The phrase "a deeper sense of letting go and a deeper sense of peace" is a clear example of my progression to increasing levels of awareness, of going more deeply within.

A second piece in my mosaic, my personal tapestry, was integrating and reinforcing all the lessons I had learned as a result of my sessions with David as discussed in the last five chapters along with my new voracious appetite for spiritual readings. I previously mentioned many of the books at the end of the "Forgive and Be Free" chapter. At this point in my journey, I kept reading and hearing all the reinforcing messages about *The Way*.

I was integrating my readings of the Holy Bible, primarily the book of Psalms, the book of Proverbs, and the New Testament with the teachings of Lao Tzu in the *Tao Te Ching* (also called *The Way*) and *A Course in Miracles*. I was taking a few classes at my church. I was reading the major works of some of the great spiritual leaders of our time. While he may not be on most people's lists, I love Jonathan Bach for his humor and insights in *Illusions: The Adventures of a Reluctant Messiah*. Thank you, David, for introducing me to many of these books and spiritual teachers.

These readings were helpful to me in exploring new territory. They were an important and a necessary foundation for my spiritual progress. However, the simple act of reading is not particularly impactful and does not necessarily lead to deeper revelations, at least in my personal experience.

The third and truly critical piece of my mosaic was the next series of sessions with David on universal truths. David taught me how to incorporate self-hypnosis into my mediations on these universal truths. I interpreted these universal truths in the context of my beliefs in a Higher Power, the Holy Spirit, my inner *self*, my God. It is always our choice. The truths are universal, and how we interpret the truths is independent of religion and spirituality.

I am now more and more aware of all the connections and coincidences that just seem to happen. It is amazing to me that my random morning readings and meditations often share similar thoughts and themes from the Holy Bible, the *Tao Te Ching*, and *A Course in Miracles*. Nothing is by accident.

When I am aware of recurrent themes, I use these themes as the focal point of my daily meditations. I was also integrating and seeing the connections with what I had been learning about, namely choosing

121

my emotions, forgiving, letting go of fear, and choosing compassion, joy, and love. During a span of three months, my meditation sessions lasted one hour every day. I was incorporating one of the tools David had taught me—self-hypnosis. I allowed my subconscious mind to lead me. I trusted my inner *self* in these meditations. In this way I was going deeper and deeper to new levels of understanding and awareness. For me, this was how I was able to connect with my inner self and very importantly, stay there for a time, be silent, listen, and hear the lessons I needed to learn.

Let us pause for a minute and reflect on what will work for you. As David has explained, whether you spend three minutes or three hours in meditation, the important point is the regular practice of taking time out for yourself, to center yourself and to hear your inner *self*. My suggestion would be to experiment with a variety of types of meditations and discover what works best for you.

Each of us weaves our own uniquely beautiful, personal tapestry with our personal colors to fit our highest and best intentions.

From my perspective, I did not get this far on my journey with a checklist and readings. I have arrived at a point of amazing self-realizations with a guide and a process that allowed me to jettison my old baggage and then move forward so that I could go deeply within to discover the touchstone of my inner *self*.

I was integrating and connecting. As a research analyst, my hallmark was to create a mosaic, and I was applying all those skills to my process of looking within, starting to trust my inner *Self*. I was seeing the interconnections and the emerging patterns, creating my mosaic.

I wrote earlier in "The Power to Choose" that learning I had control over my emotions was the final frontier. That was true at that point in my journey. It was truly what I felt then. As I went more deeply within, I started to realize that there was no such thing as the final frontier in the spiritual dimension. The possibilities are infinite. As Jesus said, "With man this is impossible, but with God all things are possible" (Matthew 19:26 NIV).

What Is My Purpose?

As I wrote in the chapter titled "Let Go and Take Control," I actually said my purpose as I came out of my trance and responded to David. I did not recognize the depth and power of what I said at the time. It took me another six months to realize I had discovered my purpose.

As you may recall, earlier in May David asked me to complete the two key sentences with the first thoughts that popped into my mind. After I completed the two key sentences, I added another insight. "From this day forward, I will use all of my talents ... all of my abilities ... all of my resources ... to help all people ... not just certain people ... all people."

My initial reaction at the time was to think, *Well, isn't that a very nice altruistic intention? Where did that come from?* I really didn't pause and reflect. I just moved on about my daily life.

This is a great example of the process of personal change and transformation. There were some changes that were instantaneous. At the same time, the increasing awareness was a progressive unfolding of learning to look within and listening to my inner self. This is yet another indication of how far I would have to travel to become aware of what my inner *self* was telling me.

Although I was unaware, David knew exactly what had happened in that earlier session. David knew I had tapped into my deepest *self*. He also knew I did not realize the full significance of this. By design, David simply steps back in his process and allows the seed to germinate so that I can make the discovery in my own way and in my own time.

On the two-hundredth day of my journey, I realized my purpose.

For the previous two months, I had been meditating on giving, loving, healing, and trusting. These meditations were largely based on the spiritually oriented sessions I had been doing with David. My readings were reinforcements of the sessions and typically became the focal point of my meditation.

That very morning, at 5:22 a.m., my meditation centered on Lesson 106 of the handbook for *A Course in Miracles*.

> *I will be still and listen to the truth.*
> *What does it mean to give and to receive?*
> *Ask and expect an answer. Your request is one whose answer has*
> *been waiting long to be received by you.*

In the silence, as I meditated, it came to me.

> *Ali*: What does it mean to give and receive?
> It means Everything to me!
> To give and to receive is my Purpose!
> It is True! It is Right! It is my Purpose!

I remembered what I had said many months ago. "From this day forward, I will use all of my talents ... all of my abilities ... all of my resources ... to help all people ... not just certain people ... all people."

Amazing. Deep inside of me, my purpose had been there all along.

The very next day, I wrote in my journal. "I recognize that I do not 'have' a purpose. I do not *know* my purpose. I *am* my purpose. I am *One* with my purpose. *Giving and receiving are One in me.*"

All those years on Wall Street, chasing the illusion of success, my life was out of sync with my true inner purpose. In retrospect, perhaps it was not so surprising I was stressed. Perhaps now I am truly on a path to bring my outer life's purpose in sync with my inner life's purpose, the only path to peace and harmony.

Indeed, my very first major initiative was to write a book. As this idea of writing a book evolved, I wrote in my journal, "My book will be a gift of my journey. The story will be a compilation of the lessons I have learned, *how* my path has evolved, what I do differently now, and what I believe now, offered as a gift, however it may help anyone and everyone. My goal in writing the book is simply living out my purpose statement."

Who Am I?

I had discovered my soul purpose, and I still ask, "Who am I?" How do I answer this amazing and profoundly simple question? How would you answer that question for yourself?

This part of my journey revealed my discovery that I did indeed have a story to tell. I did know the answer to this profound question, and I always have.

As I was flying back home from a Chicago business trip, I wrote in my journal,

On the plane, I am thinking about the lessons I have learned. David had challenged me to think about what I would say in a speech to Wall Street colleagues. Traveling at 30,000 feet is ideal to gain perspective and inspiration. It comes to me. My speech to my colleagues on Wall Street is one question: Do you know who you are and where you are going and why you are here?

Yes, you are all intelligent, smarter than average. You are all very good at trading, math, sales, closing deals, research, analytics, models, etc. You are all very good at making money.

And, who are you? If you don't know who you are, how can you be a good husband/wife/partner/friend? How can you be happy with yourself?

After I landed in Cleveland, reality set in on my drive home. I did not truly know how to answer this question. I had learned many lessons so far on my journey, and yet if I could not answer this question, I did not yet truly know the story I had to tell. I realized I had further to go on my journey.

One of the instructions in "The Messiah's Handbook" in *Illusions*, by Richard Bach, is as follows:

> *Sometimes the simplest questions are the most profound. Where were you born? Where is your home? Where are you going? What are you doing? Think about these once in a while and watch your answers change.*

As I reflect on this instruction, I suddenly realized that I was making a speech to myself.

Who am I? I had come far enough in my journey to understand that I was not defined by my history and my life circumstances. A typical response in the past and the expected social response was to state my name, where I lived, my business, my title, and family members.

I was discovering that I was a soul. I had awakened to my soul purpose. Many months earlier David asked me, "Do you believe you have a soul?" I paused and reflected, so my answer would be a considered opinion and respected the deep nature of the question.

I answered, "Yes, I do believe I have a soul." David turned the table and gave me permission to ask him the very same question.

In response David said, "No, I don't believe I *have* a soul." There was a long pause. Then he said, "I believe I *am* a soul. Big difference. Our body is a vehicle for our soul to interact with other souls here on this physical plane. And we are here to learn life lessons and soul lessons."

One evening after David and I had finished a meeting to help me prepare for the upcoming Hay House Writer's Workshop Conference, our conversation turned to spirituality and the question of "Who am I?" We were brainstorming. More accurately, I was brainstorming, and David was guiding me. At exactly the right moment, David said "Right now … How will you complete this sentence: I am …?"

I went blank for a nanosecond, and from somewhere deep within me, it came. "I am Light. I am brilliant, incandescent Light!" Ah, there was my answer. I think back and recall my answer to David after my session to connect with my Higher Power. "I have changed because

127

now I can see the Light." Indeed, I can see the Light within me. I am pure Light.

From a practical point of view, this revelation did not really enter into any hypothetical speech I might give to colleagues on Wall Street. At the same time, there was a confidence and a profound centering that I experienced when I realized I *Know* my purpose. I *Know* I am a soul, and I *Know* my soul is pure Light.

I was ready to let go of the thoughts of "I am not good enough." It did not really matter to me what other people might think or whisper. I was gaining the courage and conviction to live my true purpose, my soul purpose.

My Daily Gratitudes Are My Path to Love

Every morning as I wake, I think of at least three gratitudes. This is a practice David suggested in my very first session. I loved the idea. This daily living of gratitude went on "The List of Ali's Changes and Choices" at the start of my journey.

The impact was cumulative and exponential. I started off with the basics. I named people in my family, close friends, and my beloved Zacharia (our pet). I expanded the scope to nature—the sky, the birds I fed every day, the beautiful and ever-changing lake I wake up to every morning. I finally moved on and was grateful for *me* and my life. Then I started to thank God for my life and all the blessings in my life. I have a short prayer I often say, which goes, "Thank you, God, for my life. I have no complaints."

That last sentence of the prayer is a zinger. Try it out!

At the deepest level of gratitude, there are no "yeah, buts." There are no complaints. In the deepest realm of gratitude, I connect with compassion, calm, peace, and unconditional love for myself and everyone. In my journal, I started to write about and to feel the love.

> I awake from my meditation, stretch, convulse, and stretch out my hands ... Here I am, world. Today, I am thankful for Me, thankful for the love I have for myself, for the love I bring to others. Thankful for the joy I have and the joy I bring to others. When was the last time I was thankful for me?

> Amazing recognition: doing and giving without expectation is living unconditional love. Wonderful feeling. Namaste.

> The power to ... love unconditionally ... I will ... I can ... I *do* love myself unconditionally. Mary, Zacharia and David are all teaching me about unconditional love.

There were also more revelations for me about truly understanding, feeling, and practicing unconditional love. For example, one morning I was meditating on forgiveness and love. I had another aha moment and texted David.

> *Ali*: I am totally focused on the emotion of love, but—strike that—and love hurts. Why am I hurting myself? Aha! Love only hurts if you have expectations. Unconditional love cannot hurt—love with no expectations, no conditions, freely offered— God's love. I am blessed to know unconditional

129

love—from Mary—from Zacharia. I will love myself unconditionally—that is what this is really all about. I come out of my meditation with a huge, deep stretch—tears running down my cheeks. Moment of truth.

David: The only true love is unconditional love. Anything else is an arrangement or an agreement. (I will love you if you do this, I will love you if you do that.) Once you love yourself unconditionally, you are able to love others unconditionally. And the oneness of the universe unfolds before you. Namaste.

Ali: A year ago I told a good friend the events of 2009 were a very humbling experience. She was surprised. At the time, I was hard pressed to explain why I was so humbled. The journey began way back then. And tonight you text "And the oneness of the universe unfolds before you." Tonight I see a beautiful spiritual lesson—not the painful lesson—the illusions I once thought. Namaste and thank you from my heart and soul.

David: Welcome home, welcome back to the you that you "know" yourself to be. You are exactly where you need to be on your journey on this physical plane. Namaste.

My amazing journey was taking me to what I already knew deep inside, who I always was at my deepest level, the real *me*. I was looking within and loving *me*.

Ali's List of Changes and Choices

This is a short list and a truly profound one for me. I am in awe of the indescribable sunrise, the awakening, the glorious sound of a soul waking up!

1. Knowing my soul purpose.

2. Knowing I am a soul.

3. Connecting with my soul as pure Light.

4. Loving myself just as I am, unconditional love, the only true love.

Reality check: In every moment of every day, am I the best person I can be? No. I am a flawed and humble person, and I am particularly humbled after my pernicious ego surfaces when I know I am not the best person I know I can be. All I can do is commit to improve and most importantly, commit to love myself more tomorrow than I do today. Now there is a bedrock of confidence and conviction because I am living my purpose and loving *myself*.

CHAPTER 10

I Am Not Special

*The weight of arrogance
is such that no bird
can fly carrying it.*

—St. John of the Cross

I am not special. Really? This will be a 180-degree turn for me. Growing up, I was taught that if I were special, I would be loved. The more special I was, the more I would be loved.

Hmmm ... wrong again.

The single key lesson of this chapter is that we are all loved. We are One. How can anyone convey the epiphany of Oneness? I do not have a good answer.

As I write this chapter, my thought is to describe the doors I opened. I tried the front door at first. The front door was locked. My mind was not open. I peeked through the side window. I tried the back door. I circled around and tried the front door again. I have always

133

been persistent, perhaps to a fault. This time with a new awareness blossoming, I thanked God for my persistence in staying on my path. Somewhere, somehow, on my journey, the house, my home, and the Oneness of the universe unfolded before me.

Over time, as we will explore in this chapter, I realized I needed to unlearn things I had been taught. I was taught to believe I was special. As the beautiful quote from St. John of the Cross says, the "weight of arrogance" is an anchor.

Realizing, experiencing that I am not special takes down barriers I have put up between others and myself. It is only as I start to free myself of arrogance and ego that I can fly. It is a powerful spiritual experience to truly believe and feel in your heart that we are, indeed, all God's children. Only then can I experience the Oneness rather than just mouthing the words.

The Front Door Is Locked

After my very first session with David that day in May, as we wrapped up, he put his hands together, bowed slightly, and said, "Namaste."

I said, "What? What did you just say? How do you spell that? What does it mean?" David explained that Namaste is an ancient salutation derived from Sanskrit that recognizes the divinity within each of us. His favorite definition is as follows:

> *There is a place inside of you*
> *in which the entire universe dwells.*
> *A place of Love, Peace and Happiness.*
> *When You are in that place in You,*
> *And I am in that place in Me,*

We are One.
Namaste.

I felt a bolt of energy so strong that I lost focus. I asked David to repeat the word and the definition at least three times. Hmm. Intuitively, I grasped the spirituality. Intellectually, I thought, "What just happened? What does it mean?"

Of course, ever the research analyst, back in my office, I Googled the word *Namaste* and read the history and etymology.

In the past, particularly in this new arena of emotions and spirituality, research and reading had rarely held lasting impact or revelations, at least for me. For example, perhaps you have read about the salutation *Namaste.* Perhaps you have heard it in a yoga class. Have you felt the vibration and the energy, the soul energy of *Namaste*? On day one of my journey, I actually felt the energy of Namaste, of Oneness. What did I do?

I said privately in my best New York accent, "We are all One? Really? I don't think so! After all, I am a former managing director and a highly successful career woman." Can you hear the arrogance in my mind? I heard and researched the phrase, and I did not accept the insight—at least not at first.

When I made another attempt, the door was still locked and bolted. A couple of months later, after a great afternoon of golf, David and I were on the nineteenth hole and the conversation took an unexpected turn. We had a brief discussion of "The Ten Characteristics of God's Teachers" from *A Course in Miracles.* The conversation was brief. I had never heard of "The Ten Characteristics of God's Teachers," much less

A Course in Miracles. David simply let it hang out there for my natural curiosity to grab onto whenever the right time for me might be.

The flow of the conversation moved deeper to a question about how I perceived myself. I had a strong, visceral reaction. David asked, "Do you know that you are not special?" I was stopped in my tracks. It had been a glorious afternoon, out in nature, enjoying a round of golf, and now this! Privately, I felt insulted. Immediately, I got defensive. I sat up straighter and challenged the question. I won't go into my bristling tirade regarding my IQ and career accomplishments. Suffice it to say that I did not get it.

David went on to suggest there is a very important distinction between being *special* and being *unique*.

My emotions were clouding my ability to hear. Derisively, I thought, *Well, here is another great example of a distinction without a difference!*

Indeed, the front door was locked. My mind was not open. My ego had a strong hold on my perception of the world and my perception of myself.

With the front door locked, I had a peak through the side window. I was witness to an amazing conversation and connection between my Aunt Mary and David.

I had asked David to visit Aunt Mary in her assisted living apartment. For the most part, I just wanted David to meet Mary since she was the person who was at the center of my purpose of caring and giving. Perhaps I could also learn something from him about how to connect at a deeper level with Mary, who had advanced dementia or Alzheimer's.

He explained ahead of time that this was not going to be a hypnosis session with Mary. Hypnosis is not effective on infants and people with Alzheimer's. David did indicate he would use his knowledge of the conscious and the subconscious mind to see if he could connect with Mary, ease her fears and frustrations, and help her find peace. Mary was in that transition state where at times she knew and often said, "I am losing my mind." Understandably, Mary was frightened. It was all the more so since she had been the primary caregiver for her mother, my grandma, through all her challenges with dementia.

Aunt Mary and David met one Saturday afternoon. It was a good day for Mary. The timing was great. I made the introductions, and we sat in Mary's comfortable apartment. I showed David the beautiful paintings Mary had done from when she took evening oil painting classes at the Metropolitan Museum of Art in New York City. I faded into the background as Mary started to talk with David and asked him questions to get to know him better. Mary was a true people person at heart, and so is David. As the conversation flowed, Mary asked David, "Where are you from?" David answered by sharing some of his history—where he was born, where he has lived, where he is now. David was also engaging Mary, tapping into where she was from.

As the conversation went on for ten to fifteen minutes, Mary came back to her initial question, "Where are you from?" and asked it again and again. After patiently answering several times, David took a different approach. David looked into her eyes intently and said, "I came from the same place you came from."

I will never forget the picture. Mary paused, reflected, sat up a little straighter, turned her head sideways to look back at David, and said, "Really? I suppose that is true."

What had just happened? It is my belief that in that moment David connected with Mary at a very deep level. David went on to say to Mary, "I came from the same place you came from, and I will return to the same place you are going." Mary took this in, reflected, and sagely nodded her head in affirmation. It was a beautiful moment in time. Mary did not ask that question again.

I left Mary and David to their private discussion, and when I returned after twenty minutes, Mary was holding a gift in her hand from David. The gift was a small speckled marble heart. David had asked Mary to hold the heart in her hand and to feel the love. He said, "The love of everyone who has ever loved you is in this heart ... now and always. And everyone you have ever loved is in this heart. Every time you hold this heart in your hand, you will remember and feel their love ... and your love."

This heart stayed on the nightstand by Mary's bed and was a source of strength and love to her in moments of anxiety ... and to me as Mary slowly slipped away into her own world.

As we drove back, David explained that he tried to tap into Mary's memory of love, the deep emotion of love and the feeling of love that is always in the subconscious, even after the conscious mind has wandered and forgotten much.

Since that afternoon I have looked for marble and sandstone hearts. I have a red sandstone heart on the altar in my third-floor writer's loft. I have given several hearts to Mary's neighbors in the assisted living wing. Many other friends I thought might benefit from a tactile and visual reminder that they were always loved also received hearts from me. Every time I pick up my red sandstone heart, I give it warmth, and I feel the warmth of love that connects us all to one another and connects us to our Higher Power, our Inner Self, our God.

Several weeks later, after my morning meditation, I texted David:

> *Ali*: I read Tao 16 "realize the source" and reread Tao 1 "this source is called darkness." New light for me. Namaste – it is the universe in you, in me, in everyone. Darkness is light! It is exactly what you said to Mary— we all come from the same place, we all return to the same place. Namaste always and forever takes on an even deeper meaning today.
>
> *David*: You are swimming into the deep end and I love it. Namaste.
>
> *Ali:* Into the deep end—not in the deep end—a journey, not a destination. I love it too! The water IS warm.

Unlocking Back Doors

In my wanderings, feeling lost, I found the back door. The challenges we all face have lessons for us. Sometimes the path meanders and has twists and turns. Every door opened to a new insight once I started to open my mind.

The journey was not all sweetness and light. At one point I was very torn. I was away from Mary for five weeks to spend the holidays with my husband and Zacharia. Dear Zacharia, our chocolate Lab, was suffering—more arthritis, more seizures, increasing incontinence— and still always loving. It was 3:00 a.m. I was up to help Zacharia go out, and I turned to my morning reading in *A Course in Miracles*, Handbook for Students, Lesson 166.

> *Yet in his lonely, senseless wanderings, God's gifts go with him,*
> *all unknown to him. He cannot lose them. But he will not look*
> *at what has been given him. …*
> *Your ancient fear has come upon you now, and justice has caught*
> *up with you at last. Christ's hand has touched your shoulder, and*
> *you feel that you are not alone.*

I related to this lesson on many levels. I had lived in Long Island; Binghamton, New York; Columbus, Ohio; Louisville, Kentucky; Washington, DC; Chicago; New York City; and now Catawba Island. I had chased the illusion of success, my senseless wanderings.

Who would possibly believe I had been homeless? Me. For a very long time, I had been spiritually homeless. I was full of self-pity and full of myself.

I had made a lot of changes. I was happier. Yet there were stress points. The shift changed me and changed my relationships. I caught myself thinking, *What is going on? How can this be happening?* I still felt a little lost or, more accurately, disoriented. I was still questioning and overanalyzing.

The answer to my question was in the title to this very lesson, Lesson 166, "I am entrusted with the gifts of God." There was my answer—trust and accept. I wrote in my journal,

> *Ali*: I will accept the gifts of God; I will offer the gifts
> of God. I will walk my path in joy and peace. Stop

thinking. Stop questioning. Stop analyzing. Just do it. Just keep walking. Trust and accept.

So this part of the journey used the back door. I let go of fear one more time. I was not homeless. I was not alone. I was finding a deeper level of faith, a community of faith. In this space of knowing that we all came from the same place, that we are never alone, and that we are entrusted with the gifts of God, I started to experience the feeling of Oneness and the warmth of coming home.

***

I tried the front door again. I was persistent. I was learning to be very patient. I was learning that the path was not linear. And in this following meditation, I found a key that opened the doors and windows into my heart and soul.

I was at least six months into the journey when I started meditating on seeing God in everyone, everything, and everywhere. This particular meditation had evolved out of a series of spiritually oriented self-hypnosis sessions on universal truths.

I immediately recognized that I easily related to seeing God in everything and everywhere. I love nature. I love gardening and bird-watching and hiking. I love the ocean and the lake. I love first light, the first calls of the birds' songs in the morning, the glorious hues of sunrises, the spectacular orange globe of sunsets, and the dramatic violets in the afterglow.

It was much tougher for me to see God in everybody. In fact, I was talking over dinner with a very good friend and said, "Imagine seeing God in everybody. You gotta be kidding me!" and I started laughing

141

cynically. It was a profoundly incomprehensible thought to me, *Everybody!* My friend laughed with me, gave me a knowing smile, and simply and gently said, "Yes, seriously. See God in everyone." Hmm. I clearly had some work to do.

My first step was to meditate on the thought, *I see God everywhere in everyone and in everything.* One morning I recognized the difference between saying everybody and saying everyone. I wrote in my journal,

> Today I recognize—I see—the difference between saying everybody and everyone. I am ONE with the world – let the oneness of the universe unfold before me. How many times has David said this to me in the months' past? In my meditation on this theme this morning, I feel so warm, so comfortable, so good. Aha—I am home. I tear up with happiness. I continue on in my meditation. I think about my Purpose—I will do good, not just for certain people, but for everyone. I realize I ignore a lot of people, people who serve me or help me. I don't know or remember their names. I IGNORE them.

> I hear the seagulls collectively cry out—loud calls, just outside my window. I feel they are applauding my recognition and my honesty with myself.

As I shared my journal entry with David later that week, he was very encouraging. He said, "That is a very aware statement. You are shaping your lens of perception. Everything is supporting your higher awareness and signaling you are on your right path."

I started focusing on everyone in my life, reaching out to everyone, caring about everyone, not just simply my close friends.

For example, on a business trip to Chicago, one of the young hotel bellhops stepped into the elevator and quickly hit his button. When he realized he hit the button for the next floor but actually needed to go two floors higher, he was very embarrassed. Immediately, the young man said, "I'll get off at the next floor."

I smiled and said, "You are fine. Push the floor you need. I am not in a hurry." I was rewarded with a wonderful smile of relief and thanks. It was a small change in focus and acknowledgment, and I realized the profound results and connectivity.

Here's another simple example. I was in a grocery line in the rush before New Year's Eve. Have you ever been in a grocery line, rushing to finish your dinner/holiday meal shopping? A senior citizen ahead of me in the checkout line had a ham. In the midst of scanning his order, the cashier noticed the large amount of juice in the casing around the ham and was concerned the meat might be bad. The elderly gentleman decided to go back to find another ham, and he was gone for some time. The cashier nervously looked to me and said, "I hope it will not take much longer."

I said, "That's fine. I know you are doing a kindness." When the man returned, he was not carrying a ham. He said the person he talked to advised him not to buy any of that particular type of ham. By the time it was my turn to check out, the cashier, the bagger, and I were trading recipes for sauerkraut, talking about sodium levels, etc. I was seeing God in everyone, practicing my lessons. It felt wonderful.

This was not the same person I had been most of my adult life. I started connecting with people, with strangers.

I remembered my Grandma's admonition, "Speak to no one—man, woman, nor child." Grandma loved me. She was trying to protect me. However, unless there is imminent physical violence (as there often was in NYC), fear is actually harmful to me, as I have learned. I was starting to shed my protective armor. My walls, which I had built up to protect myself and to keep people at a distance, were coming down.

My barriers were coming down. I no longer desired to put distance between others and myself. I was opening my heart to all people, not just certain people. I did my best not to judge, compare, or contrast.

At our essence we are all the same. We are all connected. This I now *Know.* I am a unique representation of God's love here on earth. I am not special. There is nothing special about me that sets me apart from others or that disconnects me from others.

And the Universe Unfolds Before Me

In January of 2011, I secured one of the very last spots (two weeks before the ship sailed) for the Hay House Writer's Workshop on an idyllic setting of the "I Can Do It! At Sea" Caribbean cruise. I had a roomie who called me "sweetie." I had not had a roommate since my college days. The first night on the cruise, I decided to sign up for a second workshop, a menu of all the Hay House authors and top talents on the cruise. I had immersed myself in a world of people and ideas that was totally new to me.

I was a sponge, soaking up all the wisdom and energy and new ways of looking at life. I was meeting people I would never have met in my prior life. If there was another investment banker on the trip, I certainly did not meet him or her. Taking two workshops, I was in classes all day every day. I never got off the ship!

On the third day after a late dinner, I was walking the top deck, soaking up the rays of the setting sun. I texted David,

> *Ali:* On a break. Have barely been outside. Taking two workshops!! Everything is new and different— learning so much. It has gotten much warmer, this much I know. [Meaning I have hardly been outside to know the weather or online to know what the markets are doing or keep up with the latest world events.]

> *David:* Congratulations. You have stepped outside your normal comfort zone and are walking your new path. Excited and open, aware without attachment. You embody the spiritual concept "Be open to everything and attached to nothing."

> You are increasing your awareness, you resonate with the Oneness around you. It is as if you are on a nature walk. And enjoying the beauty of what IS. Listening, looking, observing, KNOWING that all is in divine right order.

> You are exactly where you're supposed to be, doing exactly what you're supposed to be doing.

Feel the Oneness, let go of any expectations, and fly …
Namaste—love and light always and forever.

Well, not to put too fine a point on it, I was cruising, not flying. Oops! There I go, a little of the New York sarcastic humor, which puts distance from the wonderful, insightful commentary.

On a more serious note, pause for a minute and reread David's text. There is a message there for all of us.

Come with me on this nature walk on the deck, basking in the warmth of the Caribbean air and the beauty of the sunset. Feel the limitless excitement of experimenting and trying new things, meeting new people, and exposing yourself to new worlds. Think of a time in your life when you may have had a similar experience.

At that moment I did indeed *Know* that I was exactly where I was supposed to be, doing exactly what was right for me. I was on my path. I was so joyous, so content, so happy. David's text captured the essence of the moment. It was an experience I felt at the deepest level of my soul.

> *I offer a prayer of thanks for you:*
> *When you are in that place in You*
> *And I am in that place in Me,*
> *We are One.*

Be with me, and feel joy and happiness as you walk your unique path.

Ali's List of Changes and Choices

On a very practical level, I looked for opportunities to send loving thoughts and prayers to friends. I also made a point of extending small kindnesses to friends and to strangers every day. Perhaps it was a smile, a tap on the shoulder, an offer to run an errand, or a proposal to take someone to church.

The very deep and life-changing spiritual lessons are as follows:

1. I was connecting with everyone. We are all the same.

2. I was coming to *Know* I was not special.

3. I was seeing God everywhere in everyone and in everything.

PART 3

PUTTING THE LESSONS INTO PRACTICE

CHAPTER 11

Lessons on Self-Talk

The difference between the almost right words
and the right word
is really a large matter—
'Tis the difference between the lightning bug
and the lightning.

—Mark Twain

Throughout my business career, I had been an analyst, and writing was integral to the practice of my art. In the past I used to say, "I hate to write." Good writing is demanding and takes an extraordinary amount of time. It has to be succinct and precise in explaining the rationale for your recommendations and persuasive in motivating the reader to take action. For example, you need good writing to execute a multimillion-dollar trade based on your advice. In this part of my journey, I have learned to love the challenge of writing and sharing. And I never use the word *hate* anymore. Read on, and I'll explain why.

I love words. Always have. I was fortunate in high school to have an English teacher who emphasized vocabulary and writing, and he made it fun. For example, one afternoon we came into our class and the buzz was that our teacher had unceremoniously dumped his ass into the small garbage can by his desk that morning. He was frustrated that the earlier class was not listening. He wanted to make a point—and quite graphically—about the difference between good writing and garbage. This teacher was a character and an inspiration to me. He was not conventional. He was passionate. He lived in Greenwich Village, and he wore a beret. That was really *out there* for me, a sheltered Long Island teenager. This English teacher conveyed his love of words and taught me to appreciate the power and the subtlety of my words. Mark Twain's quote is a testament to his legacy of teaching English, at least in my memory.

Early on in my career, I had the opportunity to be responsible for investor relations in a regional bank. One of my responsibilities was to write the company's annual report. In my role as an analyst, I was adept at critiquing and dissecting the annual reports of other companies. Then I had the challenge of writing an annual report myself. Every time I thought we were close to finalizing a major section of the report, my boss would go through and edit every sentence, every word. It was excruciatingly painful and time-consuming. When the annual report was published and I was able to reflect sanely on the process and the feedback, I could see the importance of each and every word and the construction of each and every sentence and how the changes significantly improved the quality and the clarity of the communication.

Another boss would read my reports and relish in saying, "Crisp it up!" Oh, jeez! My friend and I would laugh after we became the victims of such advice and exclaim, "What are we creating? A salad?" A little derisive humor helped to slough off the bad feeling that the report was not quite good enough.

When it was my turn to be the boss, I put every analyst who worked for me through the same excruciating process. I would say, "This is a very good report. I really like your recommendation, *but* ..." I would then go on to point out what was said and not said, what was said that was clear and what was not clear. I might ask the analyst to question his or her word choice and to tighten up the logic.

I was proud of my high standards of excellence in communication. I was teaching my craft to the up-and-coming analysts. I may have learned the techniques, and yet I had not realized or learned the emotional lessons. This was another good example of how I was unaware of my emotions and of other people's feelings.

***

As I focused more on people and emotions, David was starting to teach me about the power my words had on my emotions and on relationship dynamics. This was a totally different slant. I learned that the laser focus I brought to bear on the written word was one thousand times more important and more powerful when it was applied to the spoken word.

NLP— Neuro-Linguistic Programming? Huh? David asked if I have ever heard of this field of study. I had not. David is a Master Practitioner of Neuro-Linguistic Programming.

My disclaimer is that I am not an expert in NLP. My story is about what I have experienced and how I feel the impact of words. For me, the words I choose make a difference in my mind, my body, and my emotions. There is a list of words and phrases that I now choose to delete and a list of go-to words and phrases.

It doesn't matter what your view and your knowledge of NLP is, at least in my opinion. I have read enough on the mental game of golf and learned enough about the power of positive affirmations from Louise Hay and others that I do believe words make a difference. My choice of words has made a very real difference in my mind-set and in the quality of my communication and relationships with others. As Mark Twain wrote, "'Tis the difference between the lightning bug and the lightning."

My Story of the Word *But*

The word *but*. Isn't this a profoundly unusual and even picky place to start to teach someone the power of the choice of words? Read on and reflect on what I learned. Reflect on what language may mean to you.

For me, learning why it made sense to eliminate the word *but* in most cases was a revelation. It was the start of a list that I continue to update and expand—words I will consciously not use. For those words I correct myself and replace the word or phrase with a message that is more precise, more positive, more respectful, or more caring.

One evening David and I were talking. It was a far-ranging strategic and philosophical conversation. After some time, David asked permission to make an observation. I said that I was open to his thoughts. David observed that I frequently used the word *but*. Really? That was news to me. Our conversation on business strategy continued. Over the course of the next hour, David quietly pointed out every single time I used the word. It was in almost every other sentence!

When I am in a deep conversation or a debate, I apparently think it is effective to start by saying something complimentary about what the other person has just said. With this technique, one can appear flattering and supportive. Then I deliver the zinger: *But ...*

David explained to me how *but* conveys a message that I am disregarding what has just been said. What was the first thing I said back to him? You guessed it. "Yes, *but* ..." We talked at some length, and I had to be frank. I admitted my behavior and language were transparent. My use of *but* said, "I really do not agree. I am dismissing or disrespecting or disregarding what you just said." Reflect for a moment on how *but* stops the flow of the dialogue.

Consider the alternative. David suggested that I consider using the word *and* in place of *but*. He suggested I try to become more aware of the times when I use the word *but* and learn how I can change the flow and the feeling of the conversation if I replace *but* with *and*. When I replaced *but* with *and*, I started to feel how I was building on the other person's points and keeping the flow of the conversation moving. *And* is inclusive and respectful of the other person's thoughts. Intuitively, I grasped the importance of this point.

I thought about all my conversations with analysts who had worked so hard on their reports, strategy recommendations, a trade idea, or an opinion on the relative value of a company's bond versus alternative investments. I typically met with the analyst to discuss his or her report, whether brilliant or mediocre. In my opinion, all reports could always be made better. At the end of our meeting, I would hand them a copy of the report with my specific comments and questions. Their report would be awash in red ink. "I love your report, but ..." I thought I was teaching. It was how I had been taught.

155

I also remembered my management training sessions on giving feedback in performance reviews. It appeared that it does not really matter how many points you cover detailing the person's strengths. When you get to the negative feedback, despite the constructive, developmental points that would enhance the employee's effectiveness, the person primarily hears the negative comments. "I think you have done a great job this year, *but* ..."

It is almost impossible to motivate people when you use the word *but*. Now I understand why motivating employees was not one of my strengths. It is very difficult to find the common ground in a discussion, a debate, or an argument when you use the word *but*. I better understood why some perceived me as critical and argumentative.

I committed that evening to be more aware of my choice of words, stop using *but*, and substitute the word *and* in those instances.

It turned out to be a lot of hard work over several months simply because using the word *but* was ingrained in my speech pattern. It was a very fun challenge, and I laughed at myself a lot. Finally, after four months of training, I had made progress, so I texted David.

> *Ali*: Changing BUT to AND reinforces being in the
> flow. "But" is like a dam blocking the flow of water.
> "And" opens the lock to life to flow like water. Amazing
> to reflect on the deep importance of the choice of just
> these two words. I am adding this to my list of changes
> I have made on this journey. Namaste.

Ali's Word Choices and Why

David and I continued to discuss how the words I chose had a very real impact on how I thought and felt. I also experienced a profound shift in my behavior and, in turn, how others responded to me.

Here is my list of words to eliminate or accentuate. I call it *my* list because I own it. In truth, David offers these suggestions to everyone because he *knows* what you say impacts how you feel and how you influence your family and friends. I will keep adding to the list. It is always a fun experience when I can share and add a couple of pointers of my own.

1. *But.* I commit to replace *but* with *and* because it helps build bridges and is more respectful of others.

2. *Hate.* I commit to never use the word *hate* because I can feel the negative emotion in my body every time I use this word. It is important to stop attacking myself. I no longer say, "I hate to write." I have reframed the thought, *It is my purpose to give, and there is great joy in sharing and writing my stories.*

3. *Struggle, tough, and difficult.* I catch and correct myself every time I use these words because I now understand that whatever I say and think becomes my reality. For years and years, I have struggled with a reverse pivot, an incorrect shifting of the weight in my golf swing. Every year my golf pro identifies exactly the same issue. After working with David in one session on golf hypnosis and visualization, I focused on what I wanted to do, correctly shifting my weight from the right foot and ending with my weight on the left foot. The reverse pivot is gone.

With all my golf buddies, I became focused on a positive mental attitude and calling myself out. I started calling my friends out when they used words like *struggle*, *tough*, and *difficult*. It got to be kind of a joke.

4. *You couldn't possibly understand.* I stopped using this phrase because it is judgmental and disrespectful to the person I am talking with. When I say to someone, "You couldn't possible understand what I was going through by commuting to NYC every week," I now see the ego in that presumption. It is also a way of putting distance between that person and me. I have used words as an emotional shield in the past. No more.

5. *I am trying.* I notice and correct these instances, at least most of the time. Starting a sentence with "I am trying" usually means I am tense and forcing something. For example, "I am trying so hard to make you understand. I am trying so hard to make sure that my dear Aunt Mary has the proper care in her assisted living apartment." Can you feel the tension? Can you sense how I am *trying* to control people, their behavior, and the outcome? I realize it is very important to stop pressing and forcing. This is yet another lesson in letting go. Letting go does not mean that I wouldn't do what I needed to do to get Mary the kind of care that she deserved. Rather it meant I would take appropriate action and then step aside emotionally and let events unfold.

6. *You make me feel.* I stop—or at least catch myself—when I think or say, "You make me feel," because I now understand that my emotions are my choices. No one can make me feel sad. The only person who can hurt me … is me.

7. *Whining.* I stop whining … for the most part. If I said I was going to do something, it was my choice. No one made me

commit to a project or an event. A good friend e-mailed me about being overcommitted. I shared with her my recent decision not to whine anymore, and she sarcastically replied, "Aren't *you* good!"

My story is that I committed to join a committee only to find out the meetings were interminable. I was whining to David about how I hated going to the meetings and about how there were so many other things I would much rather be doing with my time. David gently coached me, "Of course, you know why you agreed to join the committee." On reflection, I realized I believed I might have something to offer the group. It was a gift, and all true gifts are given in unconditional love. I had a choice, and I chose to offer a gift. So then and there I decided to stop whining.

I went back and reread the chapter titled "The Power to Choose" one more time and stopped whining.

8. *I can't believe.* I commit to never saying, "I can't believe," for a couple of reasons. First, sometimes the phrase focuses on a person. "I can't believe he or she is doing this." This is a thinly veiled excuse for saying, "I don't like what the person is doing," or for questioning the person's motivation. This is the trap of reacting rather than choosing my emotion. Second, sometimes the phrase is focused on an event. Of course, I can believe it is happening. There are no coincidences.

I believe everything happens for a reason. I am committed to accepting everything and everyone. It is all good.

9. *Splendiferous.* At least once a week, I intentionally use this word because it resonates with my feeling of the joy of living. Saying, "Have a splendiferous day!" is infectious in spreading the joy and awe of life to my family and friends. I smile, and invariably, they smile as well. As I wrote in the chapter "The Power to Choose," this word came from somewhere deep within me as I emerged from my first session with David. It is *my* word, my world. And of course, it is for everyone.

10. *I deserve all joy.* I say this affirmation often because it is powerful and loving and because it reinforces the new respect I have for myself. This is the affirmation that spontaneously came to me one evening on the deck of the Hay House "I Can Do It!" cruise. I will always remember the moment. I had been in classes for eight hours, and I was walking the top deck. The sun was setting. The sky was brilliant with oranges and yellows, and the Caribbean breeze was soft and warm. I breathed deeply, and there it was. "I deserve all joy!" I texted David later that evening and said, "I am transforming from 'How can I be so lucky?' to 'I deserve all joy!'"

Whenever I say this affirmation, I smile and feel the joy and love of being me. Try it on for size, and say this to yourself. I hope you smile too.

What words would you add to this list? Write them down right now. Make your own list of words that you will choose to eliminate or accentuate.

Have a splendiferous day!

CHAPTER 12

Lessons from Business

Remembering that I'll be dead soon is the most important tool I've
ever encountered to help me make the big choices in life.
Because almost everything—all external expectations,
all pride, all fear of embarrassment or failure—
these things just fall away in the face of death,
leaving only what is truly important.

—Steve Jobs

Loss has both a personal and a professional dimension. With all the mergers and acquisitions I have lived through in the span of a thirty-year career in banking, I know loss is an ongoing fact of professional life. I survived the debacle of one of the largest bank failures of the early 1980s. Many of my very good friends were let go or took early retirement. I survived the reorganization of the FDIC-rescued bank with new leadership at the top and at least three more major reorganizations. Continental Bank was ultimately acquired by the then Bank of America. Next, Bank of America was acquired by Nations Bank and emerged as the new Bank of America. I have had great new opportunities. I have been *lateralled*. I have risen and reinvented myself again and again.

We all have had to deal with loss in our professions. It could be that you were fired or demoted or asked to move to another office/location. Maybe your boss was fired or reassigned or a colleague who sat in the cubicle next to you for years decided to move on or was asked to leave.

Change is everywhere in the business world. Plants are closing, and functions are being outsourced. You or someone in your family or acquaintance—your husband, son, daughter, significant other, brother, sister, Mom, Dad, best friend, or long-term business associate—has had to deal with the emotions that inevitably surface at these times.

The emotions are often raw and always very real. In times of turmoil such as this, exactly how does one actually choose his or her emotions? This is my story of how I learned to deal with being fired. In large part, I am drawing on all the work I did in learning how to choose my emotions and learning how to let go.

***

After I left Wall Street, I was very fortunate to be appointed to a reconstituted board of directors that had a new legislative mandate to oversee a major, state-owned insurance company that had the monopoly on workers' compensation in the state. All of the facts are a matter of public record since the agency is a publicly owned and constitutionally mandated business. It is a very large business with revenues of more than $2 billion and an investment portfolio of more than $19 billion. This board position stands out as an exceptionally rewarding and fulfilling experience. The experience was rewarding because I was able to bring my considerable expertise to bear in the areas of investment policy and board governance and assist in the turnaround of a very important service to all the workers in the state. It was also a fulfilling experience because I learned so much from my new colleagues and friends on the board. We did not always agree on specific issues, but we all pulled together with the best interests of the organization at heart.

And ... I was fired. The winds of political change ultimately determined that three other board members and I, who all served at the will of the Governor, were not confirmed to serve out our second term in office. The four of us had been reappointed in the summer by the current Governor to serve a second term as members of the Board of the BWC; however, we had not been confirmed by the Senate. Come November, there was a change in leadership for the great state of Ohio. All governor-appointed board memberships were up in the air.

You've heard people say, "It's nothing personal." How does it feel? How do you manage your mind and your emotions so that you stay focused, centered, and truly in control of your emotions rather than handing your emotions over to another person or to the politics of the moment?

I will share my journal entries from this process because it was a very personal and powerful learning experience for me. Rather than clinically writing about my reflections of what happened and how I felt, I am bringing you into my reality, sharing my texts and my journal entries.

In late November, following the elections in Ohio, I texted,

> *Ali*: A little bummed—only the best Board position ever. Not for sure but the governor-elect appears to be signaling that the 4 of us will not be confirmed in

the new terms we have been serving for the past six months, after completing our initial three year terms. Another new beginning—the new year is piling up with them. Namaste

I gnawed on this feeling all day, and the next morning I wrote,

Ali: Reflecting this morning on realism and fear. Realize I have let fear creep in. Working on love and strength of love to face reality without fear. I am SAFE and secure.

David: When one door closes, another opens. Be like water and flow.

Ali: Ah … water was the key in my Tao reading this morning. Amazing!

David: Welcome to the Oneness. Come on in the water is warm. Namaste.

Ali: You won't believe this—literally soaking my feet in very warm water for a pedicure. How funny is this—Ha!!

David: Breathe in the Oneness and know you are safe and unconditionally loved, forever and always. Namaste.

David was reminding me and repeating to me key phrases from earlier sessions. I was doing small things like pedicures to "treat myself right," one of the key insights from the very first session. Besides, Thanksgiving was that week.

It was a roller-coaster ride over the next several weeks. Nothing specific was happening, just lots of rumors, intrigue, and conjecture. I had seen this movie before. Rumors always seem to proliferate and fan the fires of fear right before most mergers or reorganizations or plant closings.

> *Ali:* The Senate did not act today on any confirmations. So it looks like it's wait 'til next Tuesday. Hard to wait AND plenty to do. Hope you are having a great day …

> *Ali*: Breaking news. I have a Senate confirmation hearing on Wednesday!!!

> *Ali*: Tao #40 "Yielding is the way of the Tao"—many meanings on many levels professional, personal. Namaste.

> *David:* Namaste my friend. Have a safe trip to Columbus, peaceful and calm and relaxed. Whatever is to happen is in divine right order, you are safe. The path unfolds before you, all you must do is walk.

There are a couple of things to notice in these texts. I was still using words like *hard* and phrases like *"You won't believe this."* My learning evolved. David knew this was a tumultuous time for me, and he was coaching me to feel the calm and trust that comes naturally when you do not resist events and simply allow and go with the flow.

Nothing happened at the confirmation meeting, and the very next week I was again on the road to Columbus for the last board meeting of the year. I had a three-hour drive, and I was primarily on country roads. I had to leave in the dark at 5:00 a.m. in winter weather. On a break to get gas, I texted,

> *Ali*: I am applying lessons every day. On the drive, the
> roads are very icy. I think the roads are "bad." Catch
> myself. The roads are about what I thought they would
> be. Just go slow—40 mph, not 60 mph. I relax my
> death grip on the steering wheel, "know" I am safe and
> secure. I start to mentally check off all the small towns
> on this now familiar route. I am good. I am safe. A year
> ago I would have arrived totally stressed. Not today!!

It was almost Christmas. Why did management so often make significant changes and layoffs just before Christmas? It is nothing personal, just business, just getting everything in order for the coming new year. Deal with it, right?

Finally, after close to eight weeks of intrigue, jumping through hoops, and continuing to focus on the business at hand, the hammer dropped. The Senate voted not to confirm the appointments by the former Governor for a second term for the four sitting board members. This was not about being *fair*. The new Governor was entirely within his prerogative regarding political appointments. This was all about navigating the rapidly changing events outside of my control.

On the morning of the events, David and I shared texts as I dealt with this significant professional loss.

> *Ali*: I am out. My appointment—and those of my three
> fellow Board members up for confirmation, have not
> been confirmed by the Senate.

> *David*: And a new chapter begins.

Ali: I have just sent a note of thanks to all my fellow board members and the senior staff.

David: I trust you are at One with everything.

Ali: Hmm … I know I get the thankfulness part. I am at peace. Not sure I get the "Oneness" lesson in today's events.

David: It's all Oneness.

Ali: I just got fired—where is the oneness in that?

David: You didn't get fired … the political parties changed. You did a great job … You know the political winds. You created change in that department. You even coached each person on change. Don't change your tune now that something didn't go your way. You KNOW the universe wouldn't close one door without opening another. You never know … with all the changes that have taken place inside of you, your future is wide open.

Take an opportunity now, to step back and assess your current situation. Be open to everything and attached to nothing. Take a fresh look with your new perspective. Be the change you want to see in the world. Choose love not fear. Nothing that is real can be destroyed. Nothing that is unreal ever existed.

Keep walking your path. And KNOW that you are never alone, that you are always loved, unconditionally, that a never ending and inexhaustible source of love and light flow through you from your Higher Power. Always and forever. You are safe.

Begin to look forward in peace and to imagine your ideal future. Begin to "future pace" your path. Read the Tao, right NOW! Namaste, my friend. There is the Oneness.

I found my copy of the *Tao Te Ching*, a gift from David very early in my journey. I had told David I was a double major at the undergraduate level in both economics and philosophy. This was a great example of the broad and intuitive role my guide played in making suggestions. David always left it open-ended. It was my choice to pursue new readings or not to. The Tao has resonated with me because it is so connected to nature. I also see the Tao and the teachings of the Bible as complementary. There are no contradictions. I texted David in response:

Ali: *Tao Te Ching*, verse 12 "The master observes the world, but trusts his inner vision. He allows all things to come and go. His heart is as open as the sky."

David: Ahhhh ... there is the Oneness indeed.

That night, I wrote in my journal, "I am calm. I accept the outcome. I am a little surprised at my lack of emotion ... and pleased simply because it signifies I am at peace. I have come a long way on my journey. Who knows what will be next!"

Who knows? One month later I signed up at the last minute for the Hay House Writers Workshop on the "I Can Do It!" Caribbean cruise.

In that workshop I expanded my horizons and opened my world to an amazing discovery of knowledge and people engaged in writing and helping others. Two months later I was writing a proposal for a book I would never have written if I was still a public official.

It was an amazing example and experience. When one door closes, another opens. Indeed.

Oops! I am getting ahead of my story. The three other board members and I said our good-byes and sent our best wishes to the staff and the continuing board. I was making calls and sending notes and saying thank you to so many people. My gifts of thanks were returned in full measure. The e-mails and the phone calls I received were a treasure chest of respect and support. My cup overflowed.

There was one unique phone call that deeply touched my heart. I missed the call from one of my favorite people whom I had come to know and respect, someone who had served as a consultant to the Board. I listened to the following voice mail message:

> As we near Christmas, I think about one or two people in my life that made the year so outstanding and so enjoyable and so memorable. You are on that very short list. I wanted to call and say thank you for your uncommon good sense and good cheer as we worked through the issues over the last three years. I will remember many of the lessons from serving you as a leader of the Investment Committee, and I will carry those lessons with me through whatever walks of life I have left. It has been great working with you.

I was stunned. I was honored for many reasons. I had the highest regard for this person professionally, and he was saying he had learned many lessons from me? I had made a positive impact on his life and on the future of the organization. In all my years of working with people and moving on, I had never received a message quite like this.

I had once been arrogant, ambitious, and unaware. I had changed. I had grown. This message was both a testament to my friend and to everyone who had the grace to say, "Thank you." It was also a wonderful recognition that I had started to understand the fulfillment that came with purpose and service. In turn, how people perceived me had changed. I was feeling good about myself. I had come a long way on my journey, and it had only been eight months.

CHAPTER 13

Lessons from Golf

You cannot become a champion without the ability
to cope with your emotions.
That is the most important factor
in becoming a winner.

—Mickey Wright

The timing was perfect! I started on my new journey in May, and the golf season was moving into high gear. I was experiencing such amazing results from my initial sessions on weight loss and stress reduction, I asked David about sessions to help me improve my golf game.

We agreed on a plan. First, I would take a few lessons from my golf pro. The next step was to work with David to program the new swing into my subconscious and to train me in guided visualization. What fun!

By way of background, I have long been serious about my game of golf. It is what I love to do when I have time for play and relaxation. I am committed to being good at it. I had been researching the game, ever the analyst. This meant taking lessons from local Pros and spending time on the practice range. I was reading and absorbing and integrating the advice from a variety of experts into my game.

Even with all the things I had done—lessons, practice, training aids, readings—I knew I could take my game to the next level by working on my mental game with David. It was one thing to try to learn by reading books and practicing. It was entirely another thing to embed it in your subconscious, to breathe it in, and to visualize it as I had experienced in my early sessions with David.

This chapter on "Lessons from Golf" is another real-life example of experiential learning, at least for me.

Lessons with the Pro

Since I had a very good working relationship with my Pro, I talked about my overall plan to work with him and then have follow-up hypnosis sessions with David. I also gave him permission to talk me through and help me practice all the changes to my swing to help give me greater control and distance.

In past golf lessons, we usually worked on one or two key changes in my swing. One or two important swing changes are typically about all a person can mentally handle in one lesson. We agreed to try a more comprehensive approach because that made sense—that is, if this hypnosis stuff really worked. My Pro was a little skeptical. I could appreciate that since I had been there myself. Now I was confident and excited.

Over the course of two golf lessons, we would focus on my setup, my swing thoughts, and the following swing changes:

1. Setup

   - Good posture, athletic stance

   - Weight on inside edge of right foot

   - Weight is right of center

   - Shoulders aligned over hips

   - Keep right shoulder back

2. Key Swing Thought: Around and Around

   - Feel the eyeball on my left shoulder, keep the eyeball on the ball.

   - Initiate with right foot/right hip, stay down, good weight transfer.

   - Accelerate through the ball.

   - Finish with belt buckle facing the target, weight on left leg.

   - Hold the finish.

At David's suggestion, based on how the subconscious mind works, we focused on what I wanted to do rather than on what I didn't want to do. How many times have you heard a player say, "I don't want to hit it in the water," only to have the ball splash? How many people hit water balls, admitting defeat or at least allowing uncertainty to affect their mind-set before they have even swung the club?

The Pro and I both knew what I was doing wrong. It had been a perennial problem. I had a reverse pivot, an incorrect weight shift. On the backswing, my weight was moving to my left foot when it really should be shifting to the back foot. Then on the downswing, my weight was moving to my right foot. This is exactly the opposite of the correct weight shift. It is a very common problem with amateur golfers.

A second issue was that I had a tendency to hit *to* the ball, not *through* the ball. Another issue was that I was not engaging the power of my full body. I primarily was swinging with my arms. I needed to bring my entire body into the swing, starting with my feet, up through the hips, and then to the larger shoulder and chest muscles.

All of the changes in the previously outlined list are very carefully worded and focused on what I wanted to do. The list itself does not mention any of my issues.

I looked at this list of swing changes. After several years of golf lessons, I still had a lot of work to do. More importantly, I have had these lessons before, and they had not stuck. I was a little chagrined. This gave me all the more reason to work on the mental game with David.

The Mind Game

In my first golf hypnosis session, I specifically reviewed with David all the pointers from my lessons with the pro as outlined previously.

David added some key elements for the mental game.

- A positive affirmation. "Every day and in every way, my golf game is getting better and better."

- A short code word, OPM, "Optimum Performance Mode," to allow my subconscious mind rather than my conscious mind to encapsulate everything on the list of setup and swing thoughts, which composed my new golf swing.

- A simple routine for every shot.

  o Take two real practice swings, not warm-up swings. There is a big difference between a warm-up swing and a real, live swing with conviction.

  o Move in, address the ball, look at the target, and look at the ball.

  o Breathe in, exhale, pull the trigger, and *GO! GO* is my new trigger word.

- Step away when necessary. Erase all doubt.

In addition, I asked David to help me with my mental concentration and focus. I am a person that is easily distracted. Some of the key thoughts David suggests are as follows:

- "Every shot is the most important shot of the game."

- "I consistently hit the ball long and straight." This thought trains my mind to focus on what I want to do rather than what I do not want to do.

- "Every putt will go in the hole."

- "Bank all my good shots." Whenever I play and have a great shot, I put it in my memory bank and call it up when I have a similar shot.

David also had me focus on the feelings and the emotions in my OPM mode. It was important to ground my feelings whenever I had a great shot. OPM was intended to merge all my technical training, my swing thoughts, my emotions, and my memory bank. Imagine that!

Playing Your Game

We were incorporating the concepts of choosing my emotions into my golf game. It is only as I write this chapter that I get the connection. The list of feelings and emotions embedded in my personal OPM included

- joy,
- laughter and humor,
- friendship and caring,
- fearlessness,
- unconditional confidence, and
- the spirit of play.

What is on your list? Write it down.

Learning from Competitive Golf

There are so many life lessons one can learn by playing golf. In these next two sections, I share a couple of my experiences. Many of the lessons revolve around letting go of a bad shot, letting go of resentment over other players' behavior, or letting go of the fear of shots over water or over sand traps. Just breathe! The mind-body connection is very clear in your golf game.

I learned from events both when I did things right, fully engaging my new mental game, and when I did things wrong, not fully controlling my negative emotions.

It was the night before the second round of the club championship. I had a slim two-stroke lead. David called and left a voice mail. "Hi, Ali. One, rock 'n' roll! Have a great time. Two, your mind is totally focused; you know exactly what you need to do. Three, you are totally in OPM. You execute easily and effortlessly. You play your best game ...today. Breathe. You are calm and relaxed. Namaste."

What a great psych talk!

I called on all of the golf sessions I had done with David—visualization, positive self-talk, focus, and commitment to the shot.

I hung in the match. I was ahead and then behind, yet I was still in the game.

On the eighth hole, I was just off the green, lying three. I focused. I was talking to myself, "I have this shot. David taught me this shot. I have practiced this shot. A seven-iron used as a putter. I can make this shot." And ... I chipped in for par. I let out an unseemly shout that people heard on all the adjacent holes. I was psyched and gaining momentum. I had evened the match!

I went on to win the club championship. I played just well enough from a pure skill perspective. It was my mental game that helped me win.

I would like to give a nod to Mickey Wright, arguably one of the greatest woman players of all time. Have you heard of her? Mickey Wright won five USGA championships during her legendary career—the 1952 US

Girls' Junior and the US Women's Open in 1958, 1959, 1961, and 1964. In total, Mickey had eighty-two victories on the LPGA Tour. This was remarkable, particularly considering her early retirement at age thirty-four because of foot problems. I chose her quote, written so many years ago, to open this chapter. "You cannot become a champion without the ability to cope with your emotions."

This quote speaks to me because I am learning what the mental game feels like. For me, it is about staying in the moment, positive images, focus, and control of my emotions. This quote is also a very nice lead-in to the next lesson I learned.

Letting Go of Resentment on the Course

I have heard this story from ladies at a couple of different courses. Sometimes it happens on a day of regular play. Sometimes it happens at the start of an important tournament. This is a story about people showing up late for a tee time. It could just have easily been about slow play or about someone who loses count of their strokes on a hole.

The situation may sound small, and it is. My playing partners were late for our tee time at the start of a tournament. I had an opportunity to really learn what I must do mentally to stay in the moment and not let other players' actions or the situation affect my game. Here is theory and practice and my reality of how I learn lessons—sometimes, the hard way.

I arrived one and one half hours before tee time. I warmed up, went to the practice range, did a little chipping, and finally practiced putting. I had time to relax and chat with a friend in the Pro Shop. Then I drove off to the first tee fifteen minutes ahead of my tee time in order to see the next to last group tee off.

I looked for the other players in my pairing. It was ten minutes before our tee time. Where were they? I called the Pro Shop and was told, "They are on the way." It was five minutes to our tee time. *Where are they?* I called the Pro Shop again and was told, "They are on the way." It was past the official tee time, and the two players were late. By the PGA Rules of Golf, I could tee off. There would be penalties for the two players as a consequence.

I counseled myself, "Be the best competitor and the most generous competitor you can be. After all, this is not the pro tour." I tried to stay loose. I called the Pro Shop again.

Resentment arose. I thought, *They know the rules. I am doing the right thing by waiting.* Yet there it was—resentment welling up deep inside of me.

The players in my pairing arrived, and we were ready to go. I was first off the tee. I proceeded to "chili-dip" my drive into the lake on the left side of the fairway just ahead of the tee. I had never done this. This was a real-life consequence of resentment.

Resentment is a form of anger and also a form of fear. This time I got to learn that letting go of resentment allows me to take control. It took me three holes—well, maybe even six more holes—to let go of my anger and regain my OPM.

I know that if this situation ever arises again, I will stay relaxed. I will stay loose. I knew at the time what I was supposed to do—breathing, shoulder rolls, shaking my fingers, staying loose and detached, controlling my emotions, staying positive. Actually doing it was the learning experience. It took me about five holes to regroup. In all honesty, the petulant little girl on the tee was not a very attractive figure. I ended up doing the right thing, and I learned a valuable lesson.

Playing for Fun and Skins

The following year David and I started to play more and more golf together on the local course. David has a very good golf game. Every time we were able to work around his client schedule and get out on the course, it was an opportunity for me to learn new lessons and to relearn lessons as I observed his mental game and as he continued to coach me on my mental game.

These texts lay the foundation of what can be learned both on and off the course.

Ali: Just shot a 40–43 for an 83 on Jekyll Island! U r great—for 2 weeks I have been cruisin' and playing golf—you have been working long hours in the cold. All you have done is celebrated with me. Namaste.

David: Sounds like you had a cool day ... 83 ... yes. I am looking forward to getting on the links with you again soon. I am so happy you are at such a wonderful state of peace ... you are now "in the flow" ... stay with it ... "anchor" it in your body.

Observe what it feels like in your chest ... your stomach ... your hands, your arms. When you are in these moments ... recognize what it feels like in your body … observe it … remember it … "anchor" it … while still being in it.

Train your neural networks and connections to recognize it and reinforce it … neuroplasticity does the rest. We will talk about that later. Namaste, my friend.

I love to review this text. There is so much in it that reinforces the lessons of the mental game. Anchor it. Feel it. Be specific on where you feel it. Then embrace the mind-body connection. Train your neural networks.

On a very practical level, here are a few highlights of the lessons I learned and those reinforced by David on the course.

1. "Bank the shot." Every time either one of us had exactly the shot we visualized, "bank the shot" instilled the memory, the muscle memory, the emotional memory, in our memory bank. I can call up that picture any time I have a similar shot with great confidence.

2. "Hold your head still." I know holding my head still is a fundamental of the golf swing. One time David took a moment to anchor my head while I swung and swung again. Then I knew what it felt like when my head was still as opposed to when there was even the slightest movement. I have anchored that feeling.

3. "How would you like to see a great birdie?" Here was visualization in practice. David was probably ten yards off the green. It was an uphill putt with a rather strong right-to-left break. I answered, "Absolutely!" We were partners in a scramble format. David sank a forty-foot birdie putt, an

awesome example of the power of the mind, an up-close-and-personal view. I *banked* the moment.

4. "How about a game of skins?" I had no idea a game of skins could be so serious and so fun. Every time David and I play, usually when it is a twosome, we play skins, and I gradually learned the rules and the strategy. A game of skins is a great way to reinforce my new emphasis on focus. Birdie, poley, greenie—how many skins are on the line? I think David holds the record with seven, although I know I have gotten five and six skins on a hole with carryovers. With these kinds of swings, you are never out of the game. The best thing is that it is a very fun game because David is always having fun, playing and working, working and playing. What is the difference?

I am now a relentlessly positive golfer. My goal is to play good golf and have fun. I have learned from my mind coach what it feels like to play with a person who is relentlessly positive, focused, and always having fun in the moment. Learning by observing; then comes learning by doing.

Have you ever had the opportunity to play with someone like that? I have had the pleasure of playing with two people like that, my Dad and David.

With my other golfing buddies, namely my girlfriends, I have something of a reputation now. It is well known that I am very careful about the words I use. I do not struggle on the course or on a particular hole. I do not think or say, "This is a tough putt." When anyone uses these words just before I am about to swing or putt, I step away and regroup. I truly love to play golf, and the other players' skill level makes no difference to me. Just please don't whine.

Well, I suppose this relentless positivity can be a little annoying. A good friend and golf buddy sent me a card as she headed south for the winter. The card read, "Always remember a positive attitude may not solve all your problems, but it will annoy enough people to make it worth the effort!" I believe the card was intended as a joke. At least I hope so.

***

I read Dr. Bob Rotella's book titled *Putting out of Your Mind* several years ago. I leafed through the book again after my golf sessions with David and read the book with new eyes and new understanding.

Dr. Rotella tells a firsthand account about doubt and the mind, specifically the mind of the great Jack Nicklaus. In a presentation to a large audience, Jack Nicklaus made the point that he has never three-putted from within five feet in the final round of a tournament. One person in the audience had the temerity to challenge and question Nicklaus's statement, specifically bringing up a situation from a tournament the month before. In Rotella's account, Nicklaus said firmly and simply, "Sir, you're wrong."

Dr. Rotella's story continues,

> But the questioning man lingered, and he approached me. "Dr. Rotella," he said, "What's wrong with Nicklaus? Why can't he just admit it? You're the psychology expert. Can you explain it?"
> I asked the man whether he played golf.
> "Yes," he said.
> "What's your handicap?" I asked.
> "About sixteen," he said.

"And if you missed a short putt on the last hole of a tournament, you'd remember it and admit it," I observed.

"Of course," he confirmed.

"So let me get this straight," I said. "You're a 16 handicap, and Jack Nicklaus is the greatest golfer ever, and you want Jack to think like you do?"

Whose mind would you rather have? For me, Rotella's story brings home the critical difference between facts, belief, and *knowing*.

In *Knowing*, there is no doubt. There is no disbelief. There is only total faithfulness. It is true in golf and true in life.

Ali's Golf Testimonial

My testimonial for David Prudhomme, written that first summer, is a fitting summary to this chapter, highlighting my perception and the results from my sessions focused on golf.

Dear David,

Golf is a passion of mine—for the fun and the exercise, the experience of nature and the joy of playing and competing. My commitment to improving my game— and having more fun—is evidenced by my hours on the practice range and a series of lessons over the past five years from several wonderful pros at area golf clubs. I felt I had the technical knowledge, or at least as much as I could absorb at my level of play.

The next level for me was to seriously work on the mental game of golf, and that is why I committed to three sessions with you.

My reverse pivot was the single most important swing correction I needed to make. While years of lessons had helped me correct a lot of elements of my grip, stance, and swing, my reverse pivot was a perennial problem.

The first golf hypnosis session on visualization was fabulous and resulted in instantaneous change. My reverse pivot is gone. After years and years of knowing what I *should* do, now I am *doing* it! That change alone got me 15 yards more off the tee, and, more importantly, eliminated a "doubt" in my swing thought and dramatically improved results—*instantaneously!*

In that session I also learned the visualization technique that pros use and that I can use on my own at any time and especially when I try to groove in new swing changes and before important matches.

The next two golf sessions were totally on focus, concentration and course management. I was *thinking* on the tee, for the critical 2nd shot, for the putt, too many thoughts going through the mind. I needed to learn how to clear my mind and *focus!*

How does one control the emotions? How does one stay in the moment? How does one clear the mind? How does one focus *and* incorporate the visualization of the shot? My sessions with you were tailored to me and my mind—focused on my new golf swing, focused on the correct weight shift and timing from right to left, incorporating all the new suggested changes from my local golf pro into our pre-talk and into the session. I now have a solid mental routine in my setup and when I address the ball.

Little did I know at the time that these sessions on focus would provide the mental toughness to help me win many tournaments.

OPM—Optimum Performance Mode. Hit'm straight and long!

I am enjoying the *game* of golf more than ever.

Joyfully,

Ali

CHAPTER 14

The Journey Continues

The spiritual journey does not consist in arriving at a new destination
where a person gains what he did not have,
or becomes what he is not.
It consists in the dissipation of one's own ignorance
concerning one's self and life,
and the gradual growth of that understanding which
begins the spiritual awakening.
The finding of God is a coming to one's self.

—Aldous Huxley

Pause for a minute and let us walk a labyrinth together. Walk the path, *your* path. We all enter at the same point and walk toward the center, and the path takes us to the left and around and then redirects us to circle back to the right, going even farther away from the center. Then we again reverse course and circle back to the left on the outer limits of the labyrinth only to come closer, still wandering and still circling. Then we are at the center of the labyrinth.

The center of the labyrinth is an opportunity to pause and reflect. We have each released old patterns of behavior and beliefs, or we have offered up prayers to God in silence to guide us on our way. We then walk exactly the same path out of the labyrinth, reflecting and receiving the wisdom of our prayers and our walking meditation.

Every time I walk a labyrinth, I learn something. Every day as I wake and say my gratitudes, I know the day holds new lessons for me as both student and teacher.

My career in corporate and investment banking spanned more than thirty years. I wandered and continued to wander successfully for another nine years.

Now I can say without reservation or hesitation that the start of my new journey that one day in May was the start of something really priceless beyond all measure. I am happier. I have found the joy in my life, and I have learned to start to love myself unconditionally.

My purpose in writing this book is to better understand myself, to share my story, and to live out my soul mission in order "to use all of my talents, all of my abilities, all of my resources to help all people, not just certain people … all people."

My story is the gift of the lessons I have learned, how the process of The Best Me NOW! has evolved for me, what I do differently now and what I *know* now. This book is offered as a gift however it may help anyone and everyone, especially you.

As David Prudhomme has said, "Change is a Constant. Growth is a Choice!"

Change happens all the time all around us. Choose not to React. Choose your Emotions. Choose your Actions. Choose Growth!

Breathe. Breathe. Breathe in light, life, joy, love, and happiness.

Always choose love over fear. Choose growth. Look inward to change yourself, and change the world you see.

Like the path of the labyrinth, my path is not a straight line. There are a lot of circles, turns, and loop-de-loops.

There are times when I regress. My ego reemerges. My demanding side and my judgmental habits creep to the surface, often unexpectedly, with the people I love. Then I go back and start at the beginning. I ask for forgiveness, forgive myself, choose my emotions, and choose love.

When I regress, David and I joke, "Go back to the chapter 'Let Go and Take Control.'" I always regroup. I now know how to regroup because David has taught me how to train my own mind.

After one such episode of backsliding and regrouping, David texted me.

> Namaste, my friend ... sounds like you have done a lot of thinking today. I love it when the wheels are turning. That means change, growth, fun ... you are on fire ... go, girl!

> You are in the perfect place to be totally at peace with what is, and write from the heart. you are there ... this is exactly what you wanted ... you have a writer's loft to write your story ... your life lessons ... what you KNOW to be true ... for you ... just a fellow traveler on the journey of life ... sharing some words of wisdom

with no expectation of how they will be received … devoid of ego and reflecting on your truest SELF. Namaste, my friend and teacher.

I had made a mistake. I had reverted back to the old behavior with someone I loved. I was forgiven. Can you feel the positive energy? Can you feel the encouragement, the gentleness of the teacher? Can you see the humility?

As my journey progresses, I continue to read voraciously. David has continued to offer up new concepts and new readings. One of the readings David has recommended is Hafiz. I am transported by *The Gift, Poems by Hafiz* (renditions by Daniel Ladinsky). One poem in particular sings to me.

Only One Rule

The sky

Is a suspended blue ocean.

The stars ate the fish that swim.

The planets are the white whales I sometimes

Hitch a ride

On,

The sun and all light

Have forever fused themselves into my heart

And upon my

Skin.

Every sign Hafiz has ever seen

Reads the same.

They all say,

"Have fun, my dear; my dear, have fun,

In the beloved's divine Game,
O, in the Beloved's
Wonderful
Game."

I think this is one of the most beautiful poems I have ever read.

"Have fun" has been a mantra I have used for much of my career. In fact, when I was interviewing for a position in Chicago very early in my career, I was asked to highlight my career objectives. I outlined three objectives. The first two I gave were very standard MBA responses. The last one was to have fun. From that day on, my new boss, one of the firm's top executives, always teased me by asking, "Are you having fun yet?"

Now after all this time, I know how to have fun. I feel the happiness and joy and fun of living every minute of every day.

Dear reader and friend, have fun!

I am defining my new path one day at a time, one step at a time. Where am I going? I do not have a definitive answer. I do not know.

What I do *know* is that as my life continues to evolve and take new directions, I will be in sync with my soul purpose, and I will be true to the me I have come to know, accept, and love.

Keep walking your path and keep breathing in life. Join hands with family and friends and coaches and trainers and guides and ministers. Let go of all illusions of success. Look within and find your path to unconditional love for yourself and for us all.

Namaste.

EPILOGUE

It has been six years since that day in May—May 3 to be exact—when I chose to take control of my life. And in that time, what has changed?

On a personal note, there have been some important life events. My dear Aunt Mary transitioned. Her black-and-white cat, Boy, has come to live with me, and he adopted me.

Then as this book was about to go to press, my husband, Doug, passed away suddenly and unexpectedly. He was far too young. It is important for me to include the eulogy I gave for Doug and to share my heartfelt thanks to the man who always supported me in all my endeavors and adventures.

> It is my honor and privilege to pay tribute to Doug, my husband and best friend of forty-four years. I would ask you, for these few minutes, to see Doug through my eyes, to hear a couple of my most precious stories, and reflect on your memories and love for Doug. It is

my fervent wish that when we leave here and gather at The Cottage, an amazing legacy of Doug's, that we will share stories of fun times together with Doug, stories of our memories of Doug, and that we will smile and laugh through our grief, play rock and roll and "Hang on, Sloopy."

Doug lived life fully. He had a passionate heart, a wonderful and sometimes wicked sense of humor, and he revered intellectual discourse—meaning he would debate anything and everything with you. And of course, he was always sure he was right!

Doug was a rich mosaic of talents and abilities. Let me paint a picture of what I saw in Doug and why I loved him so.

I loved Doug, the quintessential entrepreneur. He always saw a new and better way to do things. As an ENTP, "The Inventor of Interesting Solutions," for those of you who are familiar with Personality Types, Doug's driving force in life was "to change the world." It began with his very first venture, American AgLand, which he started in the 1980s. It carried through to his latest venture, MARTmenu. Doug always saw a new way, an original way to improve upon how things were done, and it was always about changing the world, to make it a better, easier place for everyone. For this, I loved him deeply.

The Doug I knew and loved was a farmer at heart. He loved the spring, the time of planting and nurturing. He

194

loved the summer, the time of watering and growing. He always knew the crop report. Doug loved the fall, the time of harvesting, the time for fulfilling the hopes for the year. The winter season—well, not so much— which is why we both loved Jekyll Island, Georgia. Doug flowed with the rhythm of the seasons and loved the changes. And for this, I loved him back.

Doug was a lover of nature and animals, especially our dogs. You will see this in the pictures of Doug with our first yellow Lab, Gus; with Chocolate Chip, Chip for short; and with dear sweet Zacharia. There was his gentleness, a kindness, caring and compassion to nurture and grow all living things. And here is Yogi with us today. They were indeed best buddies. On our memorial cards is a picture of Doug and Yogi on Driftwood Beach in Jekyll Island, painted as a gift by our talented friend and artist Stephen Rothwell. I saw the love Doug had for our pets, for all of nature, and for this I will love him forever.

Doug easily and naturally engaged people. He connected with everyone he met. He cared deeply about the people who helped us, who kept the yard up, who cleaned the house, about the waiters, waitresses, hostesses and bartenders, about friends and business associates. His compassion and connection for people from all walks of life was evident. He was a humble man, never arrogant, always telling stories to teach, to tease, to poke others to grow and improve. And for this, too, I loved him.

Doug was a dreamer in a different way than many might understand. This quote from T. E. Lawrence puts it very well. "All men dream, but not equally. Those who dream by night in the dusty recesses of their minds, wake in the day to find it was vanity. But the dreamers of the day are dangerous men, for they may act on their dreams with open eyes, to make them possible."

When you see the pictures of The Cottage as it was before, when we were honored to preserve the family legacy of his great-grandfather Charles Holt and his grandfather William Holt, and as you see it now, you will see Doug the dreamer and doer as I saw him and loved him.

Doug was equally passionate about politics. Yes, he was progressive, a liberal, some might say. He was passionate about the welfare of everyone, not just the privileged few. Doug did his research, was relentlessly analytical and challenging and appreciated those qualities in political commentators and people in public service. I saw this passion in Doug as yet another manifestation of how he wanted to work to make a better world for everyone. And yes, even when we might have some differences of opinion, I loved him for his keen intelligence, sincerity, and conviction and for having the best interests of others at heart.

Doug was a dedicated golfer. He loved to play the game, to improve his game, to help other people learn the game. He was a good winner and a good loser. He just loved to compete, to joke, to have fun, to be out in nature. I shared his passion for the game of golf.

Doug grew up on this lake, spending all his summers here at The Cottage. Looking out at the lake from The Cottage, from the time he was a young boy, he dreamed big.

Thank you, Doug. I love you forever and always.

On a professional note, there have been some very important life-changing choices. I have invested my time and resources to be trained, and I am now a Certified Stress Management Specialist as an affiliate of From Stressed to Best and also as an MBTI-Certified Practitioner.

I am now a Personality Type Coach and Stress Reduction Consultant working with individuals, groups, and corporations to:

- Discover your unique Personality Type.
- Identify your most developed and most effective mode of operating, your Best Mode, and your least developed and least effective way of operating, your Stress Mode.
- Develop your unique Personal Action plan to reduce stress and improve every relationship in your life, both personally and professionally.

In the framework of Personality Type (which is totally nonjudgmental and celebrates everyone's unique strengths), I am an INFJ, "The Persistent Counselor," who is using all the strategic and analytical skills honed during thirty years in business to help people reduce their everyday stress. I am now living my soul purpose to use all of my talents and abilities to help all people, not just certain people.

I have also been trained by Brendon Burchard, and I am a Certified High Performance Coach. The High Performance Coaching framework is broader than the traditional life coaching approach of setting goals and bringing accountability. It is all about coaching people to succeed beyond the standard norms consistently over the long term. People know they are high performers when they live their lives with the ongoing feeling of full engagement, joy, and confidence. I am bringing the joy, as Brendon Burchard so often says, to other people learning how to live their best lives and how to live from their best selves.

Looking within, I am more grounded in the new me. I am more confident in the new me. I am more passionate about pursuing my soul purpose to serve others.

I have found my new voice, and I raise my voice in prayer and thanksgiving with joy.

You *can* do it. Be happy *now*, not tomorrow, not next week, not when you have *this* … or achieve *that*. Be Happy NOW!

Keep walking.

Namaste.

ACKNOWLEDGMENTS

How in the world does a book come into *being*? All I know from my experience is that there are probably two times ... no, a gazillion times more perspiration and persistence than inspiration. That is exactly why I am deeply grateful to everyone who has supported me and assisted me on this journey.

Many thanks to the entire team at Balboa Press for your guidance and expertise. You were always there for me, encouraging and supporting me and sharing how you have helped many new authors travel this path.

A heartfelt thank-you to my editor, Donna M. Lueke. You gave me new inspiration to move forward. You "de-italicized" me and corrected my grammar, and most of all, you helped me share my story with a cleaner story line. There is amazing wisdom, insight, talent, and art in all you bring as my editor. You are an accomplished author, poet, and photographer. It is an honor that you made the time to work with me. We are on this journey together ... forever.

I offer love and gratitude to all my family who have loved and supported me … and criticized me, rightfully so. I have learned from you all—Grandma, Mary, Bill, Mom and Dad, Janet, Ricky, Jac and Gary, and Doug. You are "my bestest," and you know exactly what that means!

My mentors and friends along the way in my business career were amazingly important in supporting and teaching me about a world that was totally new to a lower-middle class kid from Long Island, New York, who did not know what she did not know and never really dreamed big. Thank you, Holland, Bill, Holly, Jan, Linda, and Mary. And dear, dear Katie, your skewering humor and brilliant insights saved me many times.

This book would not have been possible without all my friends and confidantes who supported and encouraged me from the start as it progressed from a one-page outline to the book it is now. We laughed and groaned together. You challenged me to be truly honest, to dig deeper, and to share more, more than even I knew I had to share. With deepest appreciation, you all mean the world to me, to the writing of my story, and to this offering to reach out to countless people who may laugh and cry with us. Thank you, Karen, Sandy, Stuart, Chris, Connie & Fritz, Diana, John, Marsha, Sarah, Jeanne, and Barb.

This book would not have been happened without David Prudhomme. You asked the question, "Have you thought of writing a book?" And you were there for me, guiding me to be patient, to be honest, to be accurate, and most importantly, keeping me focused, reminding me that writing and publishing my book was a journey and a gift to be given unconditionally. I created deadlines, and you always simply asked, "Now what is really important to you, Alison?"

Your guidance and inspiration for this journey and your input in the realization of this book are appreciated beyond measure. Thank you for the masterpiece of your creation, "The Best Me NOW!," a powerful framework that you artfully delivered—nothing short of brilliant!

David, I am so grateful and appreciative of everything you have done that it is difficult to put into words how much it means to me. Please see every page of this book as a tribute and acknowledgment of the light you have lit to rekindle my inner spirit.

APPENDIX

Ali's List of Changes and Choices

The curious paradox is
that when I accept myself just as I am,
then I can change.

—Carl Rogers

Ali's list of changes and choices provides an early overview of the scope of my transformational process. The list of changes and choices goes from the very simple to the profound. What is important— and the book explains the how and why—is that these changes were instantaneous, evolutionary, and reiterative.

All of these changes evolved one step at a time. Sometimes I went off the path. Sometimes I had to learn the lesson over and over. I persevered. I had to learn patience. In fact, I had a lot to learn.

It took a lot of time, and in retrospect, it took no time at all! When I allowed it to flow and did not force it, it just happened. It was easy. It was natural. It was wonderful beyond words.

When you read this list, it is important to remember that there is a process working and supporting this transformation. My guide and my mind coach, David, is there every step of the way, introducing new ideas, new books, and shifts in perception, encouraging, supporting, challenging, cheering, and sharing.

Body

1. Eat a healthier diet—less dairy, less pasta, less bread. Eat foods that have been alive, and avoid processed foods. For example, one day I choose not add half-and-half in my coffee.

2. Lose weight—thirty pounds.

3. Drink less wine. Enjoy wine to connect with people, not to hide from people or situations.

4. Get my hair cut on a regular basis rather than my former last-minute and irregular scheduling.

5. Stop a long-standing habit of biting my nails. A French manicure is a celebration and the start of caring for my hands and nails on a regular basis

6. Take better care of my body, and provide for regular massages as an important part of my new routine of caring for myself rather than as a treat or a reward.

7. Continue with a cardio and weight regimen. It is now part of the routine of caring for me.

8. Learn Mindful Hatha Yoga at a local YWCA.

9. Reading and meditating every morning is now the way I choose to start my day. I used to start my day with the Weather Channel, CNBC, and the *Wall Street Journal.* "What will the weather be for my commute? What is the breaking news in the market? Oh shit, what do I have to deal with now?"

10. Read ... voraciously. The floodgates of my inquiring mind are reopening in a new dimension. Read the Bible—the book of Proverbs, the book of Psalms, and the New Testament. Read the *Tao Te Ching* and *A Course in Miracles.* Read Rumi and Hafiz, the great Sufi poets. *All* of this is new to me.

11. Integrate more music into my life and much less TV. Music lifts my spirit and my soul. I started buying and playing Steven Halpern CDs, such as *Chakra Suite* and *Music for Sound Healing.* I started going to local concerts, and if I am going by myself, that is okay.

12. Control my mind, training my mind to dismiss echoes, to focus, to center myself, and to stay in the present.

13. Increase my use of the word *splendiferous.* This is *my* word, my world!

14. Let go. I am not clinging. I learned to let go of my attachment to my dear Aunt Mary, to my beloved chocolate lab, Zacharia, to a terrific board experience. My experiences—and these souls—will always be with me.

15. Use *and* rather than *but.* Go with the flow. Accept things.

16. Eliminate the phrase "You make me sad, angry, or happy." "You make me" is the signal that I have given emotional control over to someone else.

17. Eliminate the word *should*. The word *could* puts judgment to the side and opens the mind to the freedom of choice.

18. Never use the word *hate*. Anger always turns inward. You only hurt yourself.

19. Stop saying, "I can't believe this is happening." Of course I can believe it!

20. Stop using words like *struggle*, *tough*, and *difficult*. What you think is what you see and what you feel. Yes, there are challenges, and I welcome these challenges and the growth that follows. I am open to all possibilities.

21. Stop using the phrase *"You couldn't possibly understand."* Don't presume. Be more respectful of the other person. Who am I to think what another person may or may not understand?

22. Eliminate the word *try*. When I *try* to do something, I feel the intensity and the tenseness in my body. Rather I must trust my inner self to guide me. Do not *force*. Do not *try*.

23. Refuse to *whine*. Simply choose what I want to do. I am not pressured to say *yes* when it does not feel right. Saying *no* is okay. I am respecting myself.

24. Win golf tournaments with my new mental game.

Spirit

25. Start every day when I first open my eyes with three expressions of gratitude. The three things I choose evolve and vary (family, friends, nature, and events).

26. My faith starts to blossom. Into the silence, I start to understand the way as Jesus and Lao Tzu taught.

27. Choose love, not fear.

28. Choose love, and let go of anger and resentment.

29. Forgive myself and everyone.

30. Love myself just as I am—unconditional love, the only true love.

31. Connect with everyone. We *are* all the same.

32. I read my personal affirmation and my statement of soul purpose on the deck of my writer's loft often.

33. I *know* I am not special. I accept the deep humility in the simple prayer, "Lord, have mercy on my soul."

34. See God in everyone and everything.

This list was started because I said to myself, "I can't believe I have made so many changes!"

Of course I can believe! I can believe all the changes I am making. This is my *new* reality. I am continuing my journey, and the list just keeps growing and growing … with me.

I can, and you can too. I invite you. I challenge you to take action. What is your next step on your path?

RESOURCES

Here is a selected list of Ali's readings and resources on her journey.

A Course in Miracles, Combined Volume (Mill Valley, CA: Foundation for Inner Peace, 2007).

Lauren Artress, *The Sand Labyrinth: Meditation at Your Fingertips* (Boston: Journey Editions, 2000).

Richard Bach, *Illusions: The Adventures of a Reluctant Messiah* (London: Arrow Books, 1992).

Richard Bach, *Jonathan Livingston Seagull* (New York: Scribner, 2006).

Calvin D. Banyan, *The Secret Language of Feelings: A Rational Approach to Emotional Mastery* (Tustin, CA: Banyan Publishing, Inc., 2003).

Henry T. Blackaby and Richard Blackaby, *Experiencing God, Day-By-Day: The Devotional Journal* (Nashville, TN: B&H Publishing Group, 1997).

Tal Ben-Shahar, PhD, *Happier: Learn the Secrets to Daily Joy and Lasting Fulfillment* (New York: McGraw-Hill, 2007).

Marcus J. Borg, *Reading the Bible Again for the First Time: Taking the Bible Seriously but Not Literally* (New York: HarperOne, 2001).

Gregg Braden, *The Divine Matrix: Bridging Time, Space, Miracles and Belief* (Carlsbad, CA: Hay House, Inc., 2007).

Gregg Braden, *Deep Truth: Igniting the Memory of Our Origin, History, Destiny, and Fate* (Carlsbad, CA: Hay House, Inc., 2011).

Richard Brodie, *The Virus of the Mind: The New Science of the Meme* (Carlsbad, CA: Hay House, Inc., 1996).

Brendon Burchard, *The Motivation Manifesto: 9 Declarations to Claim Your Personal Power* (New York: Hay House, Inc., 2014).

Colin T. Campbell, PhD, with Campbell II, MD, Thomas M., *The China Study* (Dallas: BenBella Books, Inc., 2006).

Joseph Campbell, *The Power of Myth with Bill Moyers* (New York: Doubleday, 1988).

Joseph Campbell, *The Hero's Journey: Joseph Campbell on His Life and Work* (Novato, CA: New World Library, Joseph Campbell Foundation, 1990).

Deepak Chopra and Fereydoun Kia, trans., *The Love Poems of Rumi* (New York: Harmony Books, 1998).

Paulo Coelho, *The Alchemist*, trans. Alan R. Clarke (New York: HarperOne, 1993).

Emilie Conrad, foreword by Valerie Hunt, *Life on Land: The Story of Continuum, the World-Renowned Self-Discovery and Movement Method* (Berkeley: North Atlantic Books, 2007).

David L. Cook, PhD, *Seven Days in Utopia: Golf's Sacred Journey* (Zondervan, MI: Zondervan, 2009).

Dr. Wayne W. Dyer, *Change Your Thoughts—Change Your Life, Living the Wisdom of the Tao* (Carlsbad, CA: Hay House, 2007).

Kahlil Gibran, *The Prophet* (New York: Alfred A. Knopf, 1970).

Malcolm Gladwell, *Blink: The Power of Thinking Without Thinking* (New York: Back Bay Books, 2005).

Michael H. Hart, *The 100: A Ranking of the Most Influential Persons in History* (New York: Hart Publishing Company, Inc., 1978).

Rick Hanson, PhD, *Hardwiring Happiness: The New Brain Science of Contentment, Calm, and Confidence* (New York: Harmony Books, 2013).

Thich Nhat Hanh, *Fear: Essential Wisdom for Getting through the Storm,* (New York: HarperOne, 2012).

David R. Hawkins, MD, PhD, *Power vs Force: The Hidden Determinants of Human Behavior* (West Sedona, AZ: Veritas Publishing, 2004).

Louise L. Hay, *Colors & Numbers: Your Personal Guide to Positive Vibrations in Daily Life* (Carlsbad, CA: Hay House, 1999).

Louise L. Hay, *Inner Wisdom: Meditations for the Heart and Soul* (Carlsbad, CA: Hay House, Inc., 2000).

Esther and Jerry Hicks, *The Vortex, Where the Law of Attraction Assembles All Cooperative Relationships* (Carlsbad, CA: Hay House, Inc., 2009).

Holy Bible, New Revised Standard Version (New York: American Bible Society, 1989).

Jean Houston, *The Wizard of Us: Transformational Lessons from Oz* (New York: Atria Books, 2012).

Arianna Huffington, *Thrive: The Third Metric to Redefining Success and Creating a Life of Well-being, Wisdom, and Wonder,* (New York: Harmony Books, 2014).

William M. Isaac with Philip Meyer, *Senseless Panic: How Washington Failed America* (Hoboken, NJ: John Wiley & Sons, 2010).

Thomas Jefferson, *The Jefferson Bible* (Lexington, KY: 2012).

C. G. Jung, *The Red Book, Liber Novus: A Reader's Edition*, ed. Sonu Shamdasani, trans. Kyburz, John Peck, and Sonu Shamdasani (New York: W. W. Norton & Company, The Foundation of the Works of C. G. Jung, 2009).

Byron Katie with Stephen Mitchell, *A Thousand Names for Joy: Living in Harmony with the Way Things Are* (New York: Three Rivers Press, 2007).

Thomas A. Kempis, *The Imitation of Christ*, trans. Aloysius Croft and Harold Bolton (Mineola, NY: Dover Publications, 2003).

The Gift: Poems by Hafiz, the Great Sufi Master, trans. Daniel Ladinsky (New York: Penguin Compass, 1999).

Love Poems from God: Twelve Sacred Voices from the East and West, trans. Daniel Ladinsky (New York: Penguin Compass, 2002).

I Heard God Laughing, Poems of Hope and Joy, trans. Daniel Ladinsky (New York: Penguin Books, 2006).

A Year with Hafiz: Daily Contemplations, trans. Daniel Ladinsky (New York: Penguin Books, 2010).

Nancy Levin, *Writing for My Life ... Reclaiming the Lost Pieces of Me* (Bloomington, IN: Balboa Press, 2011).

Bruce H. Lipton, PhD, *The Biology of Belief, Unleashing the Power of Consciousness, Matter and Miracles* (Carlsbad, CA: Hay House, Inc., 2011).

Max Lucado, *Grace for the Moment: Inspiration for Each Day of the Year* (Nashville: Thomas Nelson, 2007).

Thomas Merton, *New Seeds of Contemplation*, (New York: A New Directions Book, 1961).

Dan Millman, *Way of the Peaceful Warrior: A Book that Changes Lives* (Novato, CA: H. J. Kramer, New World Library, 1984).

Barbara Bernard Miller, *Mighty Inspiration: Love Letters from God* (New York: Eloquent Books, 2009).

Stephen Mitchell, *Tao Te Ching: A New English Version* (New York: HarperPerennial, 1992).

Stephen Mitchell, *The Gospel According to Jesus: A New Translation and Guide to His Essential Teachings for Believers and Unbelievers* (New York: HarperPerennial, 1993).

Stephen Mitchell, *The Second Book of the Tao* (New York: The Penguin Press, 2009).

David Mutchler and Elizabeth Beau, *Fourteen Inches to Peace; Seven Simple Steps to Move from Your Head to Your Heart* (Bloomington, IN: Balboa Press, 2012).

Maria Nemeth, PhD, *The Energy of Money: A Spiritual Guide to Financial and Personal Fulfillment* (New York: Ballantine Wellspring, The Random House Publishing Group, 1999).

Paul Pearsall, PhD, *Toxic Success: How to Stop Striving and Start Thriving* (Maui, HI: Inner Ocean Publishing, Inc., 2002).

Karl Pillemer, PhD, *30 Lessons for Living: Tried and True Advice from the Wisest Americans* (New York: Plume, 2012).

Rachel Naomi Remen, MD, foreword by Dean Ornish, *Kitchen Table Wisdom: Stories That Heal* (New York: Riverhead Books, 1996).

Cheryl Richardson, *The Unmistakable Touch of Grace: How to Recognize and Respond to the Spiritual Signpost in Your Life* (New York: Free Press, 2005).

Richard Rohr, *Falling Upward: A Spirituality for the Two Halves of Life* (New York: Jossey-Bass, A Wiley Imprint, 2011).

Gretchen Rubin, *The Happiness Project: Or, Why I Spent a Year Trying to Sing in the Morning, Clean My Closets, Fight Right, Read Aristotle, and Generally Have More Fun* (New York: Harper, 2011).

Don Miguel Ruiz with Janet Mills, *The Four Agreements: A Toltec Wisdom Book* (San Rafael, CA: Amber-Allen Publishing, 1997).

Ruth E. Schneider and David S. Prudhomme, *From Stressed to Best: A Proven Program for Reducing Everyday Stress* (Port Clinton, OH: MW Press, 2014).

Robin S. Sharma, *The Monk Who Sold His Ferrari, A Fable About Fulfilling Your Dreams and Reaching Your Destiny* (New York: HarperCollins Publishers, 1999).

Michael Sorkin, *Too Big to Fail: The Inside Story of How Wall Street and Washington Fought to Save the Financial System—and Themselves* (New York: Viking, 2009).

The Dalai Lama with Sophie Stril-Rever, *My Spiritual Journey: Personal Reflections, Teachings, and Talks*, trans. Charlotte Mandell (New York: HarperOne, 2010).

Eckhart Tolle, *The Power of Now: A Guide to Spiritual Enlightenment* (Novato, CA: New World Library and Namaste Publishing, 1999).

Stuart Warner, *Jock: A Coach's Story*, foreword by Bill Reed, (Nicholasville, KY: Wind Publications, 2010).

Alan Watts with the collaboration of Al Chung-liang Huang, *Tao: The Watercourse Way* (New York: Pantheon Books, 1975).

John Weir, *Golfers Guide to Mental Fitness: How to Train Your Mind and Achieve Your Goals Using Self-Hypnosis and Visualization* (Orlando: Mental Golf Academy Press, 2014).

Melissa Gayle West, *Exploring the Labyrinth: A Guide for Healing and Spiritual Growth* (New York: Broadway Books, 2000).

Macrina Wiederkehr, *sevensacredpauses: Living Mindfully/Through the Hours of the Day* (Notre Dame, IN: Sorin Books, 2008).

Gary Zukav, *The Seat of the Soul* (New York: Free Press, 2007).

ABOUT THE AUTHORS

Alison Lanza Falls climbed the corporate ladder to heights few women have achieved as managing director at BankAmerica Securities on Wall Street with the prestigious global certification of CFA Chartered Financial Analyst). Alison became intimately acquainted with stress.

As an INFJ Personality Type, "The Persistent Counselor," Alison turns all the strategic and analytical skills honed over thirty years in corporate and investment banking to helping people reduce their everyday stress and improve every relationship in their lives, both personally and professionally.

As a Certified High Performance Coach, Alison works with business professionals to teach them how to consistently live their best lives, fully engaged with joy and with confidence, by helping them discover in themselves the habits of and hallmarks of high-performing people.

Alison also serves on corporate and nonprofit boards as an independent director with expertise in finance, governance, and strategic planning. Her leadership on corporate governance and investment policy is highly respected from her service on the Ohio Bureau of Workers Compensation board of directors and as chair of the governance committee and vice chair of the investment committee from 2007 to 2010. Alison served as the Chair of the Board of United Way of Greater Toledo from 2005 to 2008 and also chaired their Finance Committee. Alison is currently a board member of the Trust for Public Land, Ohio.

Learn more at AlisonLanzaFalls.com.

***

David S. Prudhomme is the founder and director of Mederi Wellness, LLC. He is the creator of The Best Me NOW! and co-creator of From Stressed to Best.

David brings a unique approach to wellness, born of his lifelong quest to understand the mind and body. His techniques are powerful and grounded in the latest research, demonstrating a proven track record with thousands of clients.

Every day he helps people "shift from where they are to where they want to be," mentally, physically, and emotionally.

David expertly integrates the most current knowledge from the sciences of the conscious and subconscious mind. His research and study of nutrition, biology, physiology, psychology, philosophy, anthropology, Western and Eastern medicine, history, spirituality, brain chemistry, physics, and engineering provide him with the vast body of knowledge needed in his wellness practice.

David is a Certified High Performance Coach, certified stress reduction specialist, Certified MBTI Practioner, diabetes motivational coach, and consulting hypnotist. He is also a master practitioner of neuro-linguistic psychology.

David is a graduate of the US Naval Academy with a BS in engineering, and he served as a Marine Corps Officer and aviator in *Desert Storm*. He has an MA in Broadcast Journalism from Boston University, and he was an Investigative Reporter for an ABC affiliate.

Learn more at www.DavidSPrudhomme.com.